HOW TO BE A GREAT INVESTOR

A Faith-Based Perspective

RULES AND STRATEGIES FOR SUCCESSFUL INVESTING

ALSO BY RICHARD EVERETT

Stock Market Wisdom
How to Invest Like a Wall Street Pro

HOW TO BE
A GREAT
INVESTOR

A Faith-Based Perspective

RULES AND STRATEGIES FOR SUCCESSFUL INVESTING

R. RICHARD EVERETT
FINANCIAL PLANNER OF THE YEAR

LIBRARY OF CONGRESS CATALOGING-IN-PUBLICATION DATA:
Names: Everett, R. Richard, Author
Title: How to Be a Great Investor: A Faith Based Perspective,
Fourth Edition
Description: Published by Intelligent Design Press, 2024. Earlier versions of this book were published in 2019, 2020, and 2021.
Identifiers: ISBN (Perfect bound) | 978-1-953625-32-8
(E-book) | 978-1-953625-34-2
Subjects: | Investment Advice | Investment Techniques | Entrepreneurial Success | Stock Markets | Value Investing |
Classification: Pending LC record pending

Disclaimer A: Any legal advice herein is offered solely as the opinion and research of the author, and it is strongly advised that any legal questions be directed to a bona fide attorney. All opinions are those of the author and do not neccessarly reflect views held by the publisher or its agents.

Disclaimer B: As with any book that deals with finance, it will always run the risk of making references to companies or technologies that have already ended up in the dustbins of history. Once-dominant brands of today can quickly be the forgotten brands of tomorrow. The author has kept the information as contemporary and up-to-date as possible up until the date of publication. However, the author recognizes that current corporate giants could completely vanish in the future.

Scripture quotations taken from The Holy Bible, New International Version® NIV® Copyright © 1973 1978 1984 2011 by Biblica, Inc.™. Used with permission. All rights reserved worldwide.

INTELLIGENT DESIGN PRESS

DEDICATION

This treatise is dedicated to Jesus (my Savior), God (my Father), and the Holy Spirit (my Guide), who led me to write this book (Romans 8:14) and helped me complete His 'master' piece (John 14:16).

And to you! May your desire to learn the craft of investing be profitable.

Seek, and you shall find.
—MATTHEW 7:7

And to my five amazing grandchildren: Zachary, Evan, Reagan, Dylan, and Ariana (my superheroes!). May the challenges you face throughout your lifetime strengthen you and make you a better person. Never allow them to defeat you.

EPIGRAPH

The market, like the Lord, helps those who help themselves.

But, unlike the Lord, the market does not forgive those who know not what they do.

— WARREN BUFFETT

CONTENTS

INTRODUCTION

Welcome to *How to Be a Great Investor—Rules and Strategies for Successful Investing.*

Why did I write this book?

The primary reason is I love to teach. I earned my degree in Christian Education from the Berean School of the Bible in the 80s. Yes, I am older—but experience, wisdom, and knowledge come with age!

I entered the investment arena full-time in 1984. With decades of working in finance under my belt, I can help you avoid some of investing's pitfalls. I have taught thousands of people just like you the fine art of investing via television, radio, magazines, newsletters, books, and in person.

Many people have complimented me over the years on my knack for taking complex subjects such as investing, stock markets, and portfolio construction and breaking them down into manageable, bite-sized parts. That is my aim for this book!

Although I retired in 2008, I still love to teach classes on investing (mostly in small group settings and at local universities). Many of my students have encouraged me to write a book on the course material I teach. They tell me over and over again that there is a substantial need in the Christian community for unbiased, biblically-based investment advice.

I must confess that at this stage of my life, I wasn't looking for something else to do. Living in paradise (southwest Florida) takes up much of my time—enjoying the sunshine, beach, and friends can wear you out. However, after several promptings from the Holy Spirit, friends, and students, I stepped out of the boat and wrote this book.

Even though I am not as old as Caleb when he asked for another mountain to climb (Joshua 14:10-12), writing this book at this stage of my life was exhilarating. I tackled this project with the same zeal and enthusiasm as I imagine Caleb did. My goal is to teach you how to become a great investor. Your success will largely depend on your actions after you have read *How to Be a Great Investor*. I can't do it for you; I can only show you the way.

You hold your financial destiny in your hands at this very moment. May the hand of God bless and guide you, and may the hand that penned this book provide you with the insight you need to become an extraordinary investor. I assume that is your goal. After all, why else would you invest your time and money in this book?

> Whatever you do, work at it with all your heart, as working for the Lord, not for human masters.
> — Colossians 3:23 (NIV)

1.

IF ONLY INVESTING
WERE EASY

On January 8, 2008, I returned home from our attorney's office with a very large check. We had just sold our investment firm. The Everett Financial Group, Inc. had been one of the largest and most successful independent investment companies in the United States. My darling wife, MarySue, asked me what I planned to do with the check; I think she felt a shopping spree coming on! I told her I planned to put it in a guaranteed money market account. The stock market was overpriced, and I felt led to put the proceeds in a safe place until better investment opportunities opened up.

As you may remember, the Great Recession began just a few months later. Using Wall Street vernacular, the U.S. economy and stock markets got *trashed*. It was a financial crisis of biblical proportions. I wish I could say I was a genius and saw the economic meltdown coming, but that would not be accurate. I'm just not that smart—better to be blessed than brilliant.

> Trust in the Lord with all your heart and lean not on your own understanding. Acknowledge Him in all your ways, and He will make your paths straight.
>
> — PROVERBS 3:5 AND 6

Allow me to digress. A few years earlier, MarySue and I had a serious discussion at our dining room table one evening. We decided to sell all our business holdings and real estate investments. We both felt it was time to downsize and enjoy life. Our timing turned out to be impeccable—God's favor is awesome!

I started my career in finance in 1984, working for a large national firm. I soon discovered that most brokerage houses are more interested in selling their investment products and less interested in their clients' financial well-being. Let's be real—these firms are publicly traded and profit-driven. Low or no profits have a dramatic impact on their share prices. When I saw those odious—and frankly ridiculous—Wall Street bonuses, I was outraged!

The CEOs' annual bonuses at Morgan Stanley, JP Morgan Chase, and Merrill Lynch were in the 20 to 25 million dollar range, their salaries as long as telephone numbers. Where does that money come from? Investors like you and me. How in the world can they call that fair and justify it to the people they profess to serve? It didn't take long for me to figure out that if I wanted to do what was best for my clients, I would have to leave the big guys behind and start my own firm. Thus, The Everett Financial Group, Inc. was born.

Now, back to my opening story…

In the spring of 2009, the Dow Jones Industrial Average[1] (the most famous and best-known stock market barometer) dipped below 7,000 for the first time since 1997—a 50% decline from its pre-recession peak. I let MarySue know my thoughts. I told her this might be a good time to invest some of the capital we had been sitting on for the past 15 months. Her response was simple and direct: "After all these years, I trust your judgment. Do what you think is best."

So, we pulled the trigger and made a bundle by buying blue-chip stocks at substantial discounts. Buying low and selling high is a terrific investment strategy; it works every time! But most people do not have the courage to invest when the outlook is gloomy. They are not familiar with the cycles of the market; they only imagine it getting worse. When you've studied the stock market and financial instruments as long as I have, you know if you buy smart and remain patient, you will do well in the long run.

I'm a value investor and a bargain hunter. I enjoy buying my Tommy Bahama shirts on eBay at 75 to 80% below their retail prices. I also enjoy buying stocks and bonds at deeply discounted prices. Thus, my favorite quote from Warren Buffett, chairman of Berkshire Hathaway, Inc. and the best investor of my generation:

> You try to be greedy when others are fearful, and you try
> to be very fearful when others are greedy.

That's how you make a bundle of money on Wall Street. At the end of 2009, our investment account was up over 50% in just nine months! To say I was deliriously happy would be an understatement.

---

1   Started by Charles Dow and Edward Jones on May 26, 1896. The DJIA is a stock market index containing 30 large U.S. publicly traded companies.

I can help you become a great investor by sharing the skills I have learned over the past 35 years. I wrote this book to demystify the investment process, dispel costly myths circulating in and around the financial realm, and blend decades of investment experience with biblical principles. Let me start by asserting that *it is biblically permissible for a Christian to invest*—not speculate or gamble—but to invest wisely.

One of my favorite (and most telling) stories in the Bible is in the book of Matthew 25:14-30 (ESV): the Parable of the Talents:

> [14]For it will be like a man going on a journey, who called his servants and entrusted to them his property. [15]To one, he gave five talents, to another two, to another one, to each according to his ability. Then he went away. [16]He who had received the five talents went at once and traded with them, and he made five talents more. [17]So also, he who had the two talents made two talents more. [18]But he who had received the one talent went and dug in the ground and hid his master's money. [19]Now after a long time, the master of those servants came and settled accounts with them. [20]And he who had received the five talents came forward, bringing five talents more, saying, "Master, you delivered to me five talents; here, I have made five talents more." [21]His master said to him, "Well done, good and faithful servant. You have been faithful over a little; I will set you over much. Enter into the joy of your master." [22]And he also who had the two talents came forward, saying, "Master, you delivered to me two talents; here, I have made two talents more." [23]His master said to him, "Well done, good and faithful

servant. You have been faithful over a little; I will set you over much. Enter into the joy of your master." [24]He also who had received the one talent came forward, saying, "Master, I knew you to be a hard man, reaping where you did not sow and gathering where you scattered no seed, [25]so I was afraid, and I went and hid your talent in the ground. Here, you have what is yours." [26]But his master answered him, "You wicked and slothful servant! You knew that I reap where I have not sown and gather where I scattered no seed? [27]Then you ought to have invested my money with the bankers, and at my coming, I should have received what was my own with interest. [28]So take the talent from him and give it to him who has the ten talents. [29]For to everyone who has will more be given, and he will have an abundance. But from the one who has not, even what he has will be taken away. [30]And cast the worthless servant into the outer darkness. In that place, there will be weeping and gnashing of teeth."

Get the point? The two servants who received the five and two talents (a talent is worth approximately 1.4 million dollars based on current values—big bucks[2]) went out and 'traded' immediately, doubling their master's money.

The wicked and slothful servant, however, was condemned by his master for not properly investing the talent entrusted to him. In fact, the contemporary English Version of verse 27 says: "You could have at least put my money in the bank so I could have earned interest on it." If the least he could have done was deposit it in a bank account,

---

2   Another Wall Street technical term.

the implication is he should have invested (traded) in more profitable financial instruments. That message is generally accepted worldwide. As far as I know, Cuba and North Korea are the only two dinosaurs left on the planet that do not believe in capitalism. Unfortunately, the people of those countries pay the price by living in poverty and greatly diminished lifestyles because of their leadership. Thus ends my one and only homily.

Check out Matthew 13:44 (the Parable of the Hidden Treasure) and 13:45 (the Parable of the Pearl of Great Price) for more examples of biblical validation of trading and investing.

I will cite numerous examples of God's multiplication power throughout this book. First, let's look at some misconceptions many investors have about Wall Street wizards, so-called "experts." I truly hope you see with new eyes and hear with new ears.

> Then Elisha prayed and said, "O, Lord, please open his eyes and let him see!"
>   — 2 KINGS 6:17 (ESV)

Reality Check #1

Let's start by facing reality. Successful investing can be difficult, not always logical, and sometimes downright treacherous. If investing were easy, everyone would be rich, and we all know that everyone is not rich. That being said, we must embrace reality and deal with it. Investing is a craft, not an exact science. No financial institution, business school, textbook, investment guru, portfolio manager, journalist, analyst, broadcaster, or media talking head has a magic formula or foolproof system for investing. If someone says they do, don't believe them. No such thing exists. That's not the world we live in. An accurate, realistic understanding of investing is the essential foundation for producing good results. Charlie Munger, former vice chairman of Berkshire Hathaway, is quoted as saying: "It's not supposed to be easy. Anyone who finds it easy is stupid." It takes know-how, wisdom, skill, intuition, sound judgment, time, and nerves of steel to be a great investor.

Reality Check #2

The financial markets and global economy are complex and chaotic. In other words, the financial markets (being subject to great sensitivity to small changes in conditions) are so unpredictable as to appear random.

At any given time, there are too many factors, forces, and variables at work to predict outcomes accurately. There are hundreds (if not thousands) of economic and political events that occur on any given day. Inflation, unemployment, pandemics, money supply, wars, and natural disasters (to name a few) can and will have an impact on your investment portfolio. That's a big problem since we cannot possibly know all things simultaneously, nor the impact of all such occurrences. Put another way, the future is unknowable with any degree of certainty.

> Here's the essential conundrum: investing requires us to decide how to position a portfolio for future developments, but the future isn't knowable.
>
> — HOWARD MARKS, OAK TREE CAPITAL MANAGEMENT

An excellent example of a complex or chaotic system is weather. Although a meteorologist may know historical patterns and current conditions, there is no possible way they can accurately predict what the weather will be in a month, year, or decade from now. Truth be told, most aren't even sure of the next few days. Another useful illustration is to imagine holding a handful of helium balloons and releasing them simultaneously.

It is impossible to accurately predict or calculate where each balloon will end up a day, week, or month from now. The best we can do as investors is to deal in probabilities, not absolutes. Probability means many things can happen, but only one will. Ugh! The reality is that uncertainty is the only certainty we will see in this life. In other words, we cannot create certainty where it does not exist; we must learn to adapt since we cannot accurately predict. Unfortunately, the world we live in is stubbornly disorderly—and only God knows what's around the corner. Which leads us to our next reality check.

Reality Check #3

Predicting the future is highly problematic.

> Predicting is very difficult, especially if it's about the future.
> — Niels Bohr, Nobel Laureate
> In Physics

Or, as the greatest philosopher of all time so astutely observed:

> Difficult to see. Always in motion is the future.
> — Yoda

In real life, no one can predict the future accurately and consistently. Just because someone was right once doesn't mean they'll be right again. Thousands (if not millions) of people make predictions each year. Some turn out to be correct; most don't. Even a broken clock is right twice a day. When was the last time you read a headline that said: "Psychic Wins the Lottery"? I'm guessing the same number of times

I've read one—never! But I recall reading this headline a few years back: "Psychic Friends Network Files for Bankruptcy." I guess they didn't see it coming! The bottom line is that the future is not ours to see; to think otherwise is intellectual dishonesty. Let's face it: investing can be challenging, counterintuitive, and just plain exasperating. The only golden rule in investing is that there are no golden rules.

You cannot simultaneously know the outcome of several economic events with exactness. Uncertainty is inherent in economics due to its complexity. In other words, you cannot know all things concurrently— nor the impact of all such events. Therefore, in plain English, the future is unpredictable, unforeseeable, and incalculable.

Reality Check #4

There is no such thing as a *sure thing*. That's especially true for the stock market. So, where do we get help? Who can we turn to for good advice? Academics? How many wealthy university professors do you know? Those of us who went to college know that much of what we are taught in school does not prepare us for the real world.

> In theory, there is no difference between theory and practice. In practice, there is.
>
> — JOHANNES LAMBERTUS ADRIANA VAN DE SNEPSCHEUT, A DUTCH COMPUTER SCIENTIST

If you think about it, most professors are only qualified to teach others to become professors. Most have never had a real job or career outside of their ivory towers. Many of these pedagogues have very little sense of how things really are. Many lack the understanding of reality that comes with experience. They are mainly idealistic theorists, not pragmatists or realists. Rarely do they encourage empirically supported investment strategies. To prove my point, here is a reality distortion on the grandest scale: According to one survey, 94% of college professors say they do above-average work in the classroom. By definition, the majority cannot outperform the average. Yes, I sound anti-intellectual, but I have good reasons. As Immanuel Kant said nearly 250 years ago, "All knowledge begins with experience." As a rule of thumb, he who can, does. He who cannot, teaches. Or, as I have been known to say: many smart people lack wisdom.

> However beautiful the strategy, you should occasionally look at the results.
> — WINSTON CHURCHILL

What happened when academics entered the investment arena? Disaster! Long-Term Capital Management, L.P. (LTCM) was one of the largest hedge funds in the world. Hedge funds are much like mutual funds (but with far less regulation) and charge much more than mutual funds—up to 2% of assets and 20% of profits if any are produced. Or, as the Wall Street joke goes, a hedge fund is really just a fee structure in search of an investor to fleece. Located in the affluent town of Greenwich, Connecticut, LTCM was led by Nobel Prize-winning economists and other academics from MIT, the University of Chicago, Harvard, and Stanford. Prior to its demise in 1998, its total worth was over one trillion dollars—nearly collapsing the global financial system. Their catastrophic losses were so bad that the U.S. Government (through the Federal Reserve) was forced to bail them out to prevent an economic meltdown!

The following excerpts are from Roger Lowenstein's terrific book, *When Genius Failed: The Rise and Fall of Long-Term Capital Management*:

The partners were not arrogant in their mannerisms or even their speech; it was more deep-seated. It was the arrogance of people who had been to Harvard and MIT—of people who really believed that they were more intelligent than others. "Do you know why we make so much money?" Greg Hawkins, one of the principals at LTCM, once asked an old friend from Salomon. "It's because we're smarter."

In the end, when it all collapsed, neither the Nobel Prize nor all the degrees mattered. In the end, their smug superiority came back to haunt them. The fund lost $1.9 billion (45% of its capital) in one month; rarely had such heady credentials met with such abysmal results. As it turned out, Long-Term Capital Management was a very short-term fund. It lasted only four years before it ended up in the trash heap of Wall Street's great ideas. You might say they were a bunch of high-IQ dimwits. Sometimes ideas can be so stupid that only intellectuals believe them. Without a doubt, smart people are capable of doing some pretty stupid things in the investment arena.

Investing is not a game where the guy with the 160 IQ beats the guy with the 130 IQ. Rationality is essential.
— WARREN BUFFETT

Very high IQ people can be completely useless, and many of them are.
— CHARLIE MUNGER

Call it the curse of knowledge; call them too smart for their own good. Whatever you call it, there is sufficient evidence of how dumb well-educated people can be. Many have little or no common sense.[3] *True knowledge is born from experience.* The trouble is, economic theories tend to be based on intellectually elegant assumptions about how the world operates, not on the messy reality in which we actually live. Often, their theories are too theoretical. To paraphrase Albert Einstein, "Theory must fit the observable facts." Truth is what stands the test of experience—not theory. Following their advice is a dignified road to starvation. I prefer experience (what actually works) over scholarship—avoid academic mugging at all costs. Or, as the old saying goes, *He who can, does; he who cannot, teaches.*

Interestingly enough, according to an article in *Forbes* magazine entitled "Keep Your CEO Out of Grad School," nearly one third of the companies on the 2002 Forbes 500 list are headed by CEOs without master's degrees. Those companies did better for their shareholders than the others on the list. But enough said. I think I have made my point. You now understand my stance on academics.

> By and large, I don't think too much of financial professors. It is a field of witchcraft.
> — CHARLIE MUNGER

> If you really want to beat the market, most professionals and academics can't help you.
> — JOEL GREENBLATT, COLUMBIA UNIVERSITY ACADEMIC, INVESTOR, FUND MANAGER, AND AUTHOR

---

3   I have no idea why they call it "common" sense when it is so rare. :)

If being smart or having a business degree were all it took, there would be many thousands of individuals and professional investors with great, long-term records. There aren't. The answer, it seems clear, must lie elsewhere.

— JOEL GREENBLATT

Where else should we consider going for investment help? The press, TV pundits, or talking heads? How many affluent journalists do you know? If they possessed clear insight or real knowledge of what was going on, don't you think they might be doing something else with their lives? Like hanging out with their friends in the Hamptons?

Ask yourself this question: why would someone who could consistently pick winners in the stock market agree to give you advice for free? Hmm. Ponder that one for a moment or two.

Reality Check #5

Financial journalists provide entertainment value—nothing more. Take Jim Cramer, for instance, host of "Mad Money." Jim is arguably one of the best-known gurus on television. According to a couple of studies done by Barron's magazine, Cramer's market calls posted a 47% accuracy rate, slightly worse than pure chance. On March 11, 2008, Cramer told a viewer not to sell his shares in Bear Stearns. Three days later, the stock tumbled from $159 to $2 a share. Ouch! That must have really hurt. Be careful of the hype; everyone is fallible. As a case in point, Jim proclaimed in February 2000 that there were ten stocks everyone should own. By 2009, all ten were out of business or had diminished to a fraction of their 2000 value.

Cramer strikes again. He advised people to buy Silicon Valley Bank stock a month before its collapse in February 2023—completely reprehensible! Never forget one of my favorite understated truisms: sometimes things do not go well.

Let's take a brief step back in time. Did you know television was invented by Philo Farnsworth, a self-taught inventor and physicist from Utah? Interestingly, several years after his infamous creation, he became disenchanted with the quality and commercial content of television, describing it as "a way for people to waste a lot of their lives." Well said, Philo. He later forbade its use in his own home! I guess that's why they call TV a *medium*—it's neither rare nor well done!

> I find TV very educational. Every time someone switches
> it on, I go into another room and read a good book.
> — GROUCHO MARX

Which brings us to…

The Bottom Line

Watching too much financial news can be hazardous to your portfolio's health.

Case in point: Several years ago, I participated in an arbitration case as an expert witness. A woman brought a case against her broker, claiming she lost money despite the stock market's enormous rise. As it turned out, this woman watched CNBC all day long. She would call her broker daily and tell him to buy the stock *du jour* mentioned by one of the featured gurus. Once the adjudicator found out her investment strategy was watching financial television, the case was thrown out. Listening to so-called "financial experts" is crazy. Investors who believe the experts who appear on CNBC aren't biased are naive. If stock market experts were true experts, they wouldn't share their expertise with you; they would buy stocks and keep what they know a secret. Here's the problem: Predictions are often reported as news. They are *not* news; they are predictions. The solution? Next time you get the urge to watch the financial networks, use the mute button.

In an ongoing study by CXO Advisory Group tracking 6,000 forecasts from more than 60 "gurus," the average accuracy was just 48%. A coin toss performed better than the typical market expert. Scary, huh? Even scarier, you can run out of money before a guru runs out of opinions.

Do you mean that if I flipped a coin, I'd have a better chance at success? Yes, that's exactly what I'm telling you.

> Prominent media journalism is a thoughtless process of providing the noise that can capture people's attention.
> — NASSIM NICHOLAS TALEN,
> *FOOLED BY RANDOMNESS*

As Michael Bloomberg, businessman, billionaire, author, and politician, has correctly said: "Most media people are ignorant and contemptuous of financial news in general." To prove his point, here are a few infamous quotes from the financial media that you would have been better off ignoring:

> "Beat the S&P with Our Five Top Ranked Funds"
> — *WORTH* MAGAZINE, AUGUST 1998

FACT CHECK: The average return of the five mutual funds they recommended was 23.17% versus 33.63% of the actual S&P 500 Index.

> "Unanimous Agreement That Business Will Be Good This Coming Year"
> — *THE WALL STREET JOURNAL* ON
> EXPECTATIONS FOR 1928

WHAT HAPPENED? A stock market crash that brought on the Great Depression.

Smart Money magazine's hot picks in December 1999 (such as AOL and Yahoo) lost 70% of their value. MCI made history in 2002 as the largest bankruptcy in the U.S. at the time.

> "Buy Stocks? No way!"
> — *TIME* MAGAZINE COVER STORY,
> SEPTEMBER 1988.

FACT CHECK: The S&P 500 Index (a stock market index tracking the stock performance of 500 of the largest companies listed on US stock exchanges) was at 268 on September 1, 1988. As I write this book, the S&P 500 is over 4000, up about 1500%. Great advice, eh?

"The Death of Equities"—*Business Week*, August 1979 cover story. I'm glad I didn't heed their alarmist warning. The Dow Jones Industrial Average was at 875. It has increased by over 3000% since the notorious article was published.

> Let blockheads read what blockheads wrote.
> — WARREN BUFFETT

Never take advice from someone who doesn't have to live with the consequences! I wouldn't say they are completely ignorant—they just have the illusion of knowledge. Here are three final examples of ineptness from the press:

The cheek of every American must tingle with shame as he reads the silly, flat, and dish-watery utterance of the man who has to be pointed out to intelligent foreigners as the President of the United States.

— THE CHICAGO TIMES ON ABRAHAM LINCOLN'S GETTYSBURG ADDRESS

"Dewey defeats Truman"

—CHICAGO TRIBUNE, NOVEMBER 3, 1948.

Janet Cooke won the Pulitzer Prize for her *Washington Post* articles about an eight-year-old boy with a drug addiction. The boy did not exist. She was later stripped of her prize.

Never let the truth get in the way of a good story.

— MARK TWAIN

Here's a true story. A number of years ago, I headed to Alaska for a much-needed vacation. One of the more interesting stops on the tour was a place called Liarsville. The Liarsville camp (near Skagway) was named after a journalist who went there after the Klondike gold rush and cooked up all kinds of tales. Journalists are supposed to be impartial. However, as we have seen since the 2016 election, they are anything but.

What about the headline from *The Jerusalem Herald* dating back to the first century A.D.?

"Jesus Can't Swim" was the lead story after His remarkable walk on water. ☺

> My grandfather told me you make more money selling
> information than you do following it. So, let that be a
> warning.
>
> — STEVE FORBES, JR
> EDITOR-IN-CHIEF OF FORBES MAGAZINE

Honestly, their purpose in life eludes me.

Let's summarize: It's crucial to have a clear understanding of the strengths and weaknesses of how the media presents their views. The quality of information is highly variable, as is their background, knowledge, and bias. Never forget that nearly everything we hear is an opinion, not necessarily a fact. Almost everything we see on TV is a perspective, not always the truth.

When I began my career in finance many moons ago, I was truly surprised and taken aback by how little was known by so many of these characters. Most of what they have to share with investors is worthless.

So, if you truly want to be a successful investor, lash yourself to the mast and plug your ears with wax to escape the deadly song of the Sirens. The press provides sensationalism, not informationalism. Lest you think I'm being unfair, I am not just picking on journalists; I'm insulting everyone in the media. Yes, I may have Empathy Deficient Disorder and can be quite snarky at times (if you couldn't tell by now)— it's a gift.

Let's get back to you. If you want to continue your quest for superior investment results, avoid stupidity by not taking these guys seriously.

Okay, I'm done rambling. Let's move on.

Want to waste money on financial newsletters? According to Mark Hulbert, editor of the *Hulbert Financial Digest,* an initial $100,000 investment in the S&P 500 Index over a 26-year period would be worth nearly $2,500,000 at the end of his tracking period. By way of contrast, a similar investment in the portfolios managed by the folks selling financial newsletters tracked by Hulbert was worth about $1,400,000. Wow, these investment newsletters turned out to be really, really expensive—$1.1 million, in fact. Unfortunately, many of those tabloids provided more noise than substance. You might be better off closing your eyes and pointing to the first stock your finger lands on in the Wall Street Journal. That could cost you less than buying a financial newsletter.

Moving on.

Reality Check #6

Economists and financial analysts are not clairvoyant. Many people assume financial analysts and trained economists can dispense insightful investment ideas. You would think these specialists could provide us with knowledge and know-how on how to become great investors. Maybe, maybe not. Let's take a closer look. Economists conduct research, collect and analyze data, monitor economic trends, and develop forecasts on various topics, including inflation, wages, employment, interest rates, etc. On the other hand, a financial analyst is a person whose job it is to assess the financial condition of a business or assets to determine if it is a sound investment. Both these professions require forecasting or predicting the future. But as we have already established, the future is unknowable with any degree of certainty. The overall economy has too many moving parts for us to be able to foresee what will happen one, three, or five years from now. How much trust would you put into next year's weather forecast?

One of the most discreditable predictions made by an economics professor was made by Irving Fisher[4] on October 21, 1929. Mr. Fisher

---

4   At Yale University. He died broke in 1947.

said, "Stocks have reached what looks like a permanently high plateau." Three days later, Black Thursday ushered in the Great Depression and a 90% decline in stock prices over the next three years.

Federal Reserve Chairman Alan Greenspan (considered one of the greatest economists of all time) is quoted as saying in 2005, "Derivatives have permitted the unbundling of financial risk." Three years later, the widespread use of derivatives sent the economy into a tailspin.

Experts have an astonishing record of failure. In 2008, the consensus from forecasters was that not a single world economy would fall into recession. During this flight from reality, it is estimated that Americans lost about 10 trillion dollars—that's $10,000,000,000,000!!! However, not one economist predicted this financial meltdown. You should be skeptical about traditional economic thinking that failed to signal or avert the crisis. At best, economics is an imprecise science. Economics is said to be the art of making common sense incomprehensible.

Get this: while accepting the Nobel Prize for Economics, Friedrich Hayek made an astonishing admission: not only were economists unsure about their predictions, but their tendency to present their findings with the certainty of the language of science was misleading and "may have deplorable effects." No matter how you look at it, that's not very encouraging.

Here is another example of ineptness: according to an analyst with the International Monetary Fund (IMF), economists have failed to predict 148 of the past 150 recessions. These guys get paid well and win Nobel

Prizes[5] even when they are wrong more than they are right. If these folks are so smart, why aren't they rich? Incidentally, I promise to be more upbeat in the following pages. Trying to make economics interesting is beyond my scope of competence. Hang in there; it will get better!

But first, one more infamous forecast made by a professional soothsayer.

David Lereah, chief economist for the National Association of Realtors, published a book in 2006 called Why the Real Estate Boom Will Not Bust. In December 2008, the Case-Shiller Home Price Index reported its most substantial decline in its history, down 18%. If that's not a bust, I don't know what is. In biblical times, this guy would have been stoned as a false prophet.

> I respect economists, but they are usually wrong.
> — PRESIDENT DONALD J. TRUMP

Researchers have found that over the past 35 years, U.S. stocks seen as sure winners by analysts have (on average) performed much worse than stocks predicted to flop. Wall Street analysts are as bad as everyone else at predicting the future. Their crystal balls seem to be a bit cloudy.

In fact, the S&P 500 companies with the lowest percentage of "buy" ratings by stock analysts were the top performers in 2018.

Trying to pick winners based on an analyst's recommendation is a waste of time. *By the time you hear about the next "hot stock,"*

---

5   Notably, Dictator Benito Mussolini (1935), Adolf Hitler (1939), and Joseph Stalin (who also went to seminary) (1945 & 1948) were all nominated for the Nobel Peace Prize. It is estimated that 50 million people died due to their reign of terror. Fritz Haber, a Nobel Prize Winner in Chemistry, is also well-known for helping to develop chlorine gas as a chemical weapon during World War I. Just goes to show you, no one is perfect, not even the Nobel committee.

it's already old news. Everyone else knows, too, and something that everyone else knows isn't worth knowing. So, let's bottom line this.

Weathermen, astrologers, fortune-tellers, analysts, economists, and media gurus all have the same odds of being right—and wrong. They are all fallible. Truth be known, forecasts aren't worth very much, and most people who take their advice don't make money in the markets. Remember, you cannot be dead sure of anything.

> I think economists, as a rule, take for granted they know a lot of things. If they really knew so much, they would have all the money, and we would have none.
> — BERNARD BARUCH, AMERICAN FINANCIER AND STOCK INVESTOR

At best, these mortals are paid guessers. When it comes to predicting the future behavior of complex systems, even experts are all but useless. Be confident that your ignorance is no greater than the experts; true experts should freely admit the limits of their knowledge, but they don't.

Remember, there is neither a magic pill nor a silver bullet when it comes to investing.

Or, as JFK said after the 1961 Bay of Pigs fiasco in Cuba, "How could I have been so mistaken as to have trusted the experts?" So, here is my first investment tip: You must think independently and be willing to be different; otherwise, you'll end up like everyone else—a mediocre or poor investor.

You must learn to ignore all the fashionable nonsense to become a great investor. Or, as Charlie Munger has astutely said, "Great investing means being aversive to the standard stupidities."

Congratulations! You made it through Chapter 1. Thanks for hanging in there. According to my watch, it is time to take a stroll down Wall Street and explore your investment options in the following chapters.

But before we do, here's a quick story:

A woman's doctor informed her that she only had six months to live. The doctor advised her to marry an economist. The woman asked, "Will this make me live longer?" The doctor answered, "No. But it will seem longer."

2.
STOCKS AND THE STOCK MARKET: A BRIEF HISTORY LESSON

On May 17, 1792, 24 stockbrokers formed a centralized exchange for the growing United States securities market. Interestingly, these two dozen financiers signed the agreement for what would later become the New York Stock Exchange on a thoroughfare only eight blocks long—Wall Street.

Today, *Wall Street* is used to describe America's financial sector and is often the center of a love-hate relationship with the general public.

There are now three major stock exchanges in the United States. The New York Stock Exchange (NYSE), sometimes called "The Big Board," is the world's largest stock exchange, handling hundreds of billions of dollars in daily trading volume. There are nearly two thousand companies listed on the NYSE, many of which are massive blue-chip corporations such as ExxonMobil, IBM, and Walmart.[6]

The National Association of Securities Dealers Automated Quotations (NASDAQ) began in 1971. This newer exchange has roughly three thousand listed companies representing around 20 trillion dollars in market value. The NASDAQ is where you'll find many of the new economy and technology stocks, such as Apple, Microsoft, and Amazon.[7]

The American Stock Exchange (AMEX) got its start in the 1800s and is the smallest of the three major exchanges. Also located in New York City, the AMEX is known primarily for trading in small-cap stocks, options, and exchange-traded funds. The AMEX is sometimes referred to as the "curb."

Why, you ask? Because they used to meet in the street to exchange securities. After several fatalities caused by crazy NYC taxi drivers, I'm guessing they wised up and moved from the street onto the curb. These guys got to move indoors in 1921 after putting up with decades of bitterly cold winds off the Atlantic Ocean. I'm not sure why it took them so long. Thus ends the one and only history lesson this book will offer.

Over the long haul, stocks have proven to be one of the best-performing asset classes. You can make loads of money in the great years and lose a substantial amount of money in the lousy years, with up years nearing 40 to 50% and negative years of 40 to 50%. The long-term average annual compound returns of the S&P 500 Index (over the past 45 years) have been about 12%. A word of caution is in order: if you

---

6   These companies are not specific investment recommendations from the author.

7   These companies are not specific investment recommendations from the author.

decide investing in stocks is the right vehicle for you and your family, make sure you have a long-term time horizon—at least five to ten years.

Warren Buffett said it best: "The market, like the Lord, helps those who help themselves, but unlike the Lord, the market does not forgive those who know not what they do."

My warning to you is to enter the investment arena cautiously. I can definitively tell you the stock markets will go up, they will go down, they will move sideways, and they will fluctuate. If you can figure out when those events will occur, you can make a bundle.

So, what exactly is a stock?

It is a "share" representing ownership in a corporation. If you buy a stock in a publicly traded company, you become a shareholder. As such, you are a partial owner and have a claim to your proportional share of the corporation's assets if they should file for bankruptcy.

For example, say a company has 100,000 shares of stock outstanding, and you purchase 1,000 shares. You now own 1% of the company. Pretty neat, huh? You can own a fraction of some of the best companies in the world and share in their profits, growth, and revenue.

Stocks are usually categorized as growth or value—as if life were really that simple!

Growth stocks are expected to have above-average increases in revenue, earnings, and business expansion. They grow at a rapid rate and imply increasing profits will follow. A few examples of growth stocks are Stamps.com, Nvidia, and Meta.[8] Value stocks, on the other hand, are perceived to trade at a price below market value based on their financial condition. In other words, they appear to be trading at a discount or as undervalued. Value stocks are typically considered less

---

8   These companies are not specific investment recommendations from the author.

risky than growth stocks. However, stay alert; change is constant on Wall Street. Today's growth stock can become tomorrow's value stock after a severe downturn.

It's not risky to buy securities at a fraction of what they're worth.

— WARREN BUFFETT

Bull markets are born on pessimism, grow on skepticism, mature on optimism, and die on euphoria. The time of maximum pessimism is the best time to buy, and the time of maximum optimism is the best time to sell.

— JOHN TEMPLETON

For those properly prepared, the bear market is not only a calamity, but an opportunity.

— JOHN TEMPLETON

What is a bull market?

Generally speaking, a bull market is a period of steadily increasing stock prices of at least 20% or more but facetiously defined as an upward movement in prices causing an investor to mistake himself for a financial genius.

What is a bear market?

A bear market is when the stock market experiences prolonged price declines of 20% or more from recent highs.

Here's our first investment principle: Your success or failure in the stock market (or any other investment) is directly proportional to the price you pay. If you overpay for your stock, it might take years to make a profit. If you buy your stock on sale at a deep discount, you have potentially less downside risk and more upside probability. In other words, money is made on the purchase, not the sale.

Yahoo shares are a great example. If you bought Yahoo in January 2000, you paid a hefty $237 per share. Fifteen months later, Yahoo was trading at $11, a 95% decline—ouch! It might take a couple of lifetimes to break even on this not-so-fortuitous trade. If, on the other hand, you purchased Yahoo when it was trading at $11, you would have had a 600% gain in less than five years! Same stock, different purchase price, entirely different outcome. A word of caution—one of the most significant risks investors face is a direct function of the price they pay for their investment!

> What is smart at one price is dumb at another.
> —WARREN BUFFETT

Putting it more bluntly, buying securities at extraordinarily high prices is economic suicide. For that reason, when a stock becomes "hot," it's generally too late to make a profit. That's when suckers buy the stock only to watch it fall. Often, they panic on the decline and sell at a tremendous loss. And that, my friends, is a scenario repeated far too often.

I am a value investor for several very good reasons—as you will find out soon enough. Hang in there with me; I promise to share the investment strategy I use to make above-average returns on my portfolio. Since I put my blueprint together a number of years ago, I have consistently produced outstanding investment returns.

However, let's not forget Chapter 1. *There is no magic formula, silver bullet, or fail-safe system when it comes to investing.* Nonetheless, by utilizing what works and eliminating what doesn't work on Wall Street, you can enhance your investment returns substantially.

My approach has worked wonderfully well for my family and me. Other investment techniques work quite well, but the strategists who employ them will have to write their own books! Before we examine my approach to investing, let's deal with dividends and why they matter.

A **dividend** is a distribution (typically cash) of a portion of a company's earnings, decided upon by the board of directors and paid to its shareholders. Dividends are usually paid out quarterly or annually. Receiving dividends is one of the ways an investor makes money. The bottom line is that a dividend is your share in the apportioned profits of a company in which you own stock.

Attractive, don't you think? Here's why dividends are so vital: First, if you are retired, they help supplement your income. Second, according to Ned Davis Research, Inc., over the past several decades, 42% of the total annual return of the S&P 500 was derived from dividends. Get the implication? Buy a non-dividend-paying stock, and you likely miss out on a ton of money.

According to the same research, dividend-paying stocks outperformed non-dividend-paying stocks over the past 40-plus years by 6% per year and with lower risk.

That's a very big deal! How big?

A gentleman approached me for investment advice in late 2009. He had a $1.2 million retirement portfolio comprising mainly of individual growth stocks and growth mutual funds, which generally do not pay dividends. Prior to the Great Recession stock market meltdown of 2007–2009, his investment account was worth $2 million.

Not only had he lost his shirt, he had also lost $800,000. One of the reasons for the 40% decline was that he was forced to sell more shares at a substantially discounted price to generate the $60,000 per year he needed to live on. Selling low is not a great investment strategy; it was wreaking havoc on his investments. To further illustrate this point, suppose I purchased a substantial number of shares of a company trading at $100 each. I plan on selling one share per month ($100) to supplement my income. Now, suppose my stock declines by 50% to $50 per share. To get my $100 per month, I must now sell two shares. I will run out of shares and money much sooner if the stock stays depressed for a prolonged period. The man was in trouble, to say the least.

Imagine working your entire adult lifetime to accumulate a good-sized nest egg, only to lose 30, 40, or even 50% of your life savings in just a couple of years. Fortunately, I was able to help guide him back to solvency. By selling what he had in his portfolio and purchasing an assortment of income-producing investments, the bleeding stopped. He could now avoid selling any shares, live off the income (still $60,000) and maintain his standard of living. $1.2 million x 5% (dividend income) equals $60,000 annually.

But here's the good news for my new best friend. His portfolio recovered sooner because he was able to stop selling things in his brokerage account at discounted prices.

Here are six additional reasons I favor dividend-paying stocks:

1. Companies that increase their dividends signal confidence in their future.
2. Buying dividend-growing stocks hedges against inflation.
3. Dividends are less taxing: 15 to 20% versus ordinary taxation.

4. Dividend-paying companies generally represent mature, stable businesses.
5. They can provide steady cash flow.
6. They have relatively solid profits.

One of my favorite personal success stories—if I may brag a moment—concerns two of the high dividend-paying stocks I bought on my shopping spree in April 2009 after the near-death experience of the stock market: AT&T (T) and Altria Group, Inc. (MO).

Because I bought both at a great price (cheap), my current dividend yield on T is 8% and 20% on MO. That's not a misprint. Since purchasing Altria, they have more than doubled their dividend payment, which pleases me to no end. More recently, in the middle of the COVID-19 pandemic, with the S&P 500 down 34%,[9] I went bargain-hunting again. Just two of the gems I picked up were Prudential Financial, with a 10% dividend yield, and MetLife, with a 6% yield. Both companies have an outstanding track record of raising their dividends every year—so the future looks bright for this retiree.

One of the secrets to entering the investing promised land is buying high-quality blue-chip stocks with solid earnings at the right (discounted) price. Get the gist?

As Peter Lynch (author, investor, mutual fund manager extraordinaire, and Andy Warhol look-alike) is quoted as saying, "The reason that stocks do better than bonds is not hard to fathom. As companies grow larger and more profitable, their stockholders share in the increased profits as dividends are raised. The dividend is such a critical factor in the success of many stocks that you could hardly go wrong by making an entire portfolio of companies that have raised their dividends for ten

---

or 20 years in a row." I don't think my new BFF would disagree with Mr. Lynch.

And finally, here are a couple of quotes from Ben Graham, the "father of value investing":

> One of the most persuasive tests of high quality is an uninterrupted record of dividend payments going back over many years.
>
>   ***
>
> The true investor will do better if he forgets about the stock market and pays attention to his dividend returns and the operation results of his companies.
>
> — BENJAMIN GRAHAM

It's time to get down to the nitty-gritty. I use a checklist or filter to narrow down my stock picks. I stay focused and disciplined. If a stock doesn't meet my criteria, I do not buy it under any circumstances. But first, here is why using an investment checklist works well for me: research published in *The New England Journal of Medicine* found that when surgical teams heeded a simple checklist (as pilots do before takeoff), patient mortality rates were cut in half, and complications fell by more than a third.

According to Dr. Atul Gawande (author of the book, *The Checklist Manifesto: How to Get Things Right),* "Any one thing at any given time might not add up to too much, but the net effect of all of it put together, especially for more effective teamwork, matters." Since most humans are not always consistent, old-fashioned checklists (like those used by construction engineers, pilots, investors, and restaurateurs) help things get done correctly and in less time.

Not surprisingly, 94% of doctors surveyed said they would want a checklist used if they were having an operation.

So, if you want to become a more efficient investor and save time, money, and energy by reducing mistakes (and if you want a better chance of getting it right the first time), checklists are the answer. As you know, it is simpler to prevent a problem than fix it.

I repeat: checklists are critical for investors.

Charlie Munger said, "I'm a great believer in solving hard problems by using a checklist."

He went on to say, "You need mental models; a checklist of procedures to help you decide."

If you are analyzing a company without an adequate checklist, you will, quite likely, make a very bad investment.

By using checklists, investors have an excellent chance of improving their investment process and formulating repeatable strategies.

Being able to invest capital with a fixed set of rules and principles is one of the keys to wealth creation. Checklists help you focus on what matters most. They also help take the guesswork and impulse buying out of the equation.

So, let's check out what makes a reliable checklist.

Investing in the stock market (or in individual stocks) can be rewarding—think Apple, Microsoft, Amazon, and Google, all with tremendous long-term returns.

Investing can also be very dangerous, especially if you don't know what you are doing—think Enron, WorldCom, and Lehman Brothers (all bankrupt companies). Investing in stocks can be rewarding or disastrous, so you must choose wisely.

As investing gets more complicated over time, unsophisticated and undereducated stock pickers are especially disadvantaged by the complexity. The more choices there are (currently 50,000 stocks traded worldwide), the more confusing things get. That's why it is as important as ever to make enlightened, well-educated choices when investing in stocks.

The good news is that when it comes to investing, simplicity trumps complexity. As you are about to discover, my checklist is not rocket science. It contains no calculus or algorithms (thank God!)— only wisdom I've gained from investing during most of my adult life. Fortunately for you, I have made many mistakes along the way so you won't have to. Here we go…

My Checklist: A Recipe for Success:

1. First and foremost, any company I buy must have earnings— period. Earnings will ultimately decide a stock's fate. If it's not making money, I'm not interested. I have no desire to speculate as to whether the company is a turnaround candidate or a probable target to be bought.
2. I only buy stocks that pay a dividend. You already know why.
3. The dividend payout must be less than 50%[10] of the company's earnings. Why? Any company paying out more than half its earnings may have a difficult time staying healthy when the next economic downturn comes—and it will come!
4. I look for companies that have increased their dividends or paid out a "special dividend." Any company that has recently increased its dividend must be optimistic about the future.
5. I do not buy any stock trading under $5 a share, which the Securities and Exchange Commission (SEC) considers a penny

---

10 Unless it is a REIT, which must pay out 90% of its earnings as dividends.

stock.[11] There must be a good reason why it's trading so low.[12] For the most part, I won't buy a stock trading under $10 a share. There must be an excellent reason for me to do so; an extreme anomaly must be present.

6. I look for stocks insiders are buying. If a corporate executive is buying shares of the company they work for, it's generally a good sign. Either they think the stock price is cheap and undervalued, or they are expecting good things to happen. Several studies have shown the profitability of tracking insider trading. Companies with insiders buying lots of their shares have managed to beat the market by an average of 7% per year over the past 50 years! *Very impressive.*

7. Along the same lines, look for companies that are buying back their shares. Why? Several studies have shown that buy-back stocks perform better over time than the main market indices. Additionally, an analysis done by Mergent, Inc. showed buy-back achievers had a lower risk profile than the Russell Midcap Value Index over one-, three-, five-, and ten-year periods. Another excellent reason to focus on share repurchase is that if a company uses its cash to buy back its shares, it must think its shares are underpriced. By reducing the number of outstanding shares, a company increases its earnings per share. The same earnings divided between fewer shares translates into more earnings per share. That could mean a higher dividend or a more attractive share price for investors.

---

11 Personally, I wouldn't give you two cents for a penny stock.

12 One Wall Street joke goes like this: "How do you make a million dollars in penny stocks? Start with two million." They are too risky for the average investor.

> When a company grows and outstanding shares shrink,
> good things happen for shareholders.
> —WARREN BUFFETT

8. A company's price-to-earnings (P/E) ratio must be lower than the S&P 500 overall market index for me to buy shares. In other words, if the P/E ratio of the S&P 500 Index is currently at 20, I would be looking for individual stocks with a P/E ratio of under 20. What is a P/E Ratio? Put simply, it is the company's stock price divided by the earnings per share. For example, if a stock trades at $100, and its earnings per share is $10, the P/E ratio is 10 (100/10 = 10). To put it another way, you pay $10 for every dollar of earnings. As a rule of thumb, the lower the P/E (but not the lowest), the more appealing the stock. Historically, low P/E stocks have consistently outperformed high P/E stocks over one-, five-, and ten-year tracking periods. By how much? Almost double!

9. Check out any recent news about the company that may affect the share price positively or negatively going forward. Boeing (BA) is a great example. The airplane maker had nothing but bad news from 2019 to 2020. And just when you thought it couldn't get any worse, it did. Trading at over $440 a share prior to the first piece of bad news, it went as low as $140 per share—a 66% decline over 18 months. The point is that the bad news kept getting worse. So, when you hear bad news about a company you're interested in buying, wait it out. Wait for a bottom or near-bottom before you jump in.

10. The price is right. I'm always on the lookout for companies that meet my specifications and are trading at "bargain" prices. How do I define a bargain?

There's a saying on Wall Street that a rising tide lifts all boats. In other words, when the market is going up over a prolonged period (a bull market), most stocks will increase in value, deserved or not. The opposite is true with a falling tide. When the stock market gets hammered, almost all stocks tend to decline in value (deservedly or not), which can create a wonderful buying opportunity and outstanding profits. As I'm writing this, I can't help but be pleased with my most recent investment decisions (March and April 2020). With a market decline of nearly 35%, I could find an incredible number of companies selling at bargain-basement prices—some of which had increased in value by as much as 40% in just over a month!!

Yes, I'm ecstatic, but it took a great deal of courage to pull the trigger when so many people thought the world would come to an end because of COVID-19. Conversely, buy the right stocks at the wrong time and you'll suffer significant losses.

> The best investments often are made in times of fear and uncertainty.
> — HOWARD MARKS

Eureka! My investment checklist in its entirety. By utilizing these ten filters, you will stack the deck in your favor. You don't necessarily have to have all ten to buy a stock, but the more, the merrier. Remember, there are no guarantees. Never lose sight of that fact. However, I can confidently say you will be better off using a checklist like the one I've just outlined than going on your gut or the advice of some guru who's here today and gone tomorrow. You substantially increase your odds of finding companies that provide predictable returns and help you become a Great Investor.

There may be a better strategy, but I'm certain that the number of worse strategies is countless. What I just gave you is worth a lot of money—and you only had to spend $15 for the book! It's a great return on investment, isn't it? Let's hope it's your first of many.

To reiterate, to be a great investor, you should operate by a set of principles or self-imposed rules that focus your attention and restrict your choices. With slavish devotion and a consistent and structured decision-making process, you will become a successful investor.

> The only time I really ever lost money was when I broke my own rules.
> — JESSE LIVERMORE,
> LEGENDARY STOCK TRADER

Before you freak out and have a nervous breakdown, all the information needed to complete the checklist can be found free of charge on Yahoo Finance. Just type in a stock's ticker symbol (a unique abbreviation used to identify a publicly traded company), and voilà—you have multiple pages of information at your fingertips on just about every company listed on the major stock exchanges. Examples of ticker symbols:[13]

LUV = Southwest Airline Co.
GM = General Motors Co.
PEP = PepsiCo, Inc.

---

13 These companies are not specific investment recommendations from the author.

Now, a very important question: Who should invest in stocks? The answer is, it depends on many factors. Good investors need to know why they are investing. Is it for growth, income, growth and income, or the preservation of capital? For how long (during what time horizon) will you be investing? One year, ten years, a lifetime?

Can you withstand market declines of 20%, 30%, or more? As an investor, you must "know thyself"[14] before putting your hard-earned money into the stock market. The beginning of wisdom is achieving an accurate picture of yourself. Will you bail if the market plummets? Investing in the stock market is not for everyone. If you're a coward, do not invest in stocks. To be a good investor, you must be patient and disciplined and completely remove emotion from the equation. Fortunately, my ancestors came from England. English people are quite stoic. We lack a great deal of emotion, which (as an investor) suits me perfectly. By the way, the reason I know I'm British is I had my DNA tested. As it turns out, I didn't evolve from a monkey. (I have always wondered: if humans came from monkeys, why are there still monkeys?)

Before some of you go bananas, let's get back to investing.

Too many people buy high and sell low. They get greedy and buy hot stocks only to get burned. Good investors know stock market declines are inevitable and see them as buying opportunities. Take one of the credit reporting agencies, for example. You may recall a massive data breach in 2017. It was estimated that as many as 150 million consumers were affected. As you might imagine, this adverse event had a devastating impact on the agency's stock price. Trading at around $140 a share prior to the bad news being made public, it quickly sank to $93—a 33% decline in just a couple of weeks. If you recognized this as

---

14 If you don't know your investment personality, go to greatinvestor.org to take the free risk analysis.

a buying opportunity (as I did), you could have made $25 a share in just eight weeks. Buy low; sell high. Put another way: *a crisis is a terrible thing to waste.* Buy damaged stocks, not damaged companies—got it? Unfortunately, the stock market is the only place where things go on sale and the customers run away.

Not only am I a value investor, but I am also an opportunist. I have made money on several such trades in my career.

> The best thing that happens to us is when a great company gets into temporary trouble—we want to buy them when they're on the operating table.
> — WARREN BUFFETT

Before we close this chapter and move on to bonds, I have eight valuable ideas to share with you to increase your investing prowess. First, a question: Initial Public Offerings (IPOs)—are they good investments? Some are, but most aren't. IPOs tend to substantially underperform over the three to five years after going public. I would strongly urge you to stay away from them.

Here is how the IPO game is played. **First**, the best offerings are generally reserved for the very high net-worth clients of the investment bankers who do the underwriting. If an IPO trickles down to the average investor, it's because no one else wanted it. The idea that a new issue will be the cheapest thing to buy among thousands of stocks is ludicrous.

What is an IPO?

An IPO is when a private company or corporation raises capital by offering its stock to the public for the first time.

Second, stocks that have performed poorly over the past three to five years generally outperform those that have done well over the previous three-to-five-year period. That must have something to do with the buy low, sell high principle. Jesus shared similar wisdom in Matthew 20:16: "So the last will be first, and the first will be last." The ancient Roman poet, Horace, gave the same investment advice over 2,000 years ago: "Many shall be restored that are now fallen, and many shall fall that are now in honor."

Third, "Hope" is not an investment strategy. The stock market doesn't care what you think or how you feel, and it doesn't know what stocks you like or what you wish would happen. The stock market doesn't even know you exist. You can't just buy a stock because your plumber mentioned it in passing and then hope it goes up while you watch it go down the drain. Here is some really bad news: the investment world does not always conform to our expectations, desires, hopes, or thoughts. Unfortunately, even sound investment decisions can lead to unfavorable outcomes in an unknown world.

I love to read; on average, I read a book a week. Most of what I read concerns investing. I scratch my head when the author makes a statement such as: "If you feel like the stock is going to go up…" or "If you think the market will go down…" What difference does it make how I feel or think? The market has no idea what I'm hoping for, thinking, or feeling. You need to make sound investment decisions and live with the consequences, good or bad. Stay calm, rational, cold-blooded, and detach your emotions when choosing an investment.

Here is another reality check: It's impossible not to lose money in the stock market at some point. No one bats a thousand. Even the best money managers make mistakes—except, of course, Bernie Madoff (pronounced made-off, as in with other people's money), who never had a down year. The problem is that he is no longer in the investment business. While serving a 150-year prison sentence for fraud, he died.

Since getting caught red-handed,[15] he didn't do much of anything except make license plates after pleading guilty to multiple securities fraud charges before his demise.

Fourth, when should you consider selling a stock? After all, there is a time to buy and a time to sell. Someone with a lot more wisdom than any of us said it this way: "There is a time to sow and a time to reap."

Here are five sell signals from one of Peter Lynch's books. Consider selling your shares:

1. **When a company changes its name.** It may be trying to hide something.
2. **When a company lowers or suspends its dividend payments.** Bad news is most likely forthcoming.
3. **If the chief executive officer (CEO) or chief financial officer (CFO) quits or resigns abruptly.** Something bad is going on behind the scenes.
4. **If the stock you own is removed from the S&P 500 Index.** There is a reason why, and it is not good. Millions of shares will be dumped in a hurry, driving the share price down considerably.
5. When there is really bad news, remember the cockroach theory: there is always more than one.

My selling advice is simple: if your stock no longer meets the criteria on your checklist, sell it. Don't hang on for dear life and hope your stock will recover. Remember, hope is a lousy investment strategy, but so is waiting to break even. If you find yourself in a hole, stop digging. Get out. Don't allow hope to triumph over reality—sell. Another reason

---

15 According to my tour guide, pistachio nuts were dyed red by the sultans of the Ottoman Empire so that their subjects could never sneak a few nuts without getting caught "red-handed"!

to sell is if a substantial number of company insiders are selling a lot (millions) of shares. They know something you don't, and generally, it's not good news.

Fifth, Spinoffs. Research[16] shows that spinoffs tend to outperform the overall stock market significantly and consistently after separation from the parent company. A spinoff occurs when a publicly traded company splits off a division and lists it as a new independently traded company on one of the stock exchanges. For example, eBay spun off PayPal in 2015. Ironically, the parent company also tends to outperform the market after the spinoff, proving that, in some cases, the parts CAN be more valuable than the whole.

Sixth, Stock Splits. Stock splits occur when a public company increases their number of shares. For example, if Apple is trading at $100 and decides to do a two-for-one split, you would now own twice as many shares worth $50. However, the underlying value of Apple or your account has not changed. So why do companies split their shares? One of the primary reasons is to make shares more affordable to small investors. It's obviously easier to purchase a hundred shares of Apple for $50 than $100. What's the big deal with stock splits? Studies over the past 100 years have proven time and time again that companies do better (sometimes a lot better) than the overall market once the stock split announcement is made. One study[17] revealed shares of split stocks (on average) outperformed the market by 8% the following year and 12% over the next three years.

---

16 *Critical Business Skills for Success*, "The Diversification Discount," Professor Michael A. Roberto

17 Done by David Ikenberry, chairman of the Finance Department at the University of Illinois

A word of caution is in order: beware of reverse splits. That's when a penny stock (explained earlier) will attempt to boost its stock price. For example, say a company's stock is trading at $2.50. If they do a one-for-four reverse split, you'll now own one-fourth of the shares at a new price four times higher. Buying a reverse split is generally a poor choice for investors. There are always good opportunities in the market; why bother with companies that play accounting tricks?

Seventh, Sympathy Plays. A sympathy play can be an opportunity to take advantage of some peculiar Wall Street Logic.

A sympathy play involves buying a stock (assuming the fundamentals are sound) after a competing company releases significant news, good or bad.

Say, for example, a large bank files for bankruptcy like Silicon Valley Bank did in 2023. The fallout was a decline in many publicly traded banks after the news hit the airwaves. Ironically, I had my eyes on a regional bank that was paying a 5% dividend but the share price wasn't tempting enough to pull the trigger, so I waited. Fortunately, my patience paid off. I was able to buy the regional bank at a 30% discount thanks to the Silicon Valley Bank collapse and my self control.

Patience (waiting for a buying opportunity) is a virtue and can be very profitable.

Here's another example. Not too long ago, a leading technology company announced a substantial increase in earnings from the previous quarter (good news), which resulted in a huge surge in its stock price and the entire NASDAQ composite index. In other words, if you owned other tech stocks, you likely profited from the positive news of just one company in the industry.

Sympathy plays can be driven by various reasons: mergers and acquisitions, surprise earnings, etc.

Eighth, Second-Level Thinking. To be a great investor, you must find an edge that average investors don't have. You'll need to think of things average investors haven't thought of, have insight they don't possess, and see things beyond the obvious. Otherwise, you'll be an average investor.

First-level thinking says, "It's a good company; let's buy the stock." First-level thinking is superficial and simplistic—the quick and easy path many investors take. But remember, investing is not supposed to be easy.

Second-level thinking, on the other hand, is deeper and more complex[18]—the road less traveled. It's critical thinking.

Before I share a couple of examples of second-level thinking from my career, let me assure you that I am not intellectually gifted. I freely admit I am not the smartest person I know. My first a-ha moment came during a business trip to Beijing 20 to 25 years ago during China's initial economic boom. I couldn't help but notice the incredible amount of construction in view from my hotel room on the thirty-second floor. As far as the eye could see, countless high-rise buildings were going up. In fact, people joked at the time that the national bird of China was the crane.

As I pondered how best to profit from what I saw for my clients, the obvious—and incorrect—answer was steel. I knew what everyone else knew: steel was essential to build large buildings. When I returned to the U.S., I turned on my computer and googled how steel is made. The answer? Coal.

---

18 Paraphrased from Howard Marks' memo, "It's Not Easy" (September 9, 2015).

I dug deeper and found out that China imported a great deal of coal from Canada. I then dug even deeper and found out which Canadian coal company exported the most to China. Bingo!

I found what turned out to be a grand slam: the company was paying a 7% dividend and was a perfect holding for my retired clients requiring income. Over the next few years, the stock tripled in value and then did a stock split, doubled, and split again. It doubled again before it was purchased at a premium by a much larger coal company. We had many very, very happy clients, to say the least.

Ignore the obvious. What everybody already knows isn't worth knowing; dig deeper. Be perspicacious, insightful, and skilled when investing your hard-earned money.

I'm reminded of a story I've heard several times over the years about the California Gold Rush during the 1800s. Although most miners fared poorly during the Gold Rush, the men and women who prospered the most were second-level thinkers. They catered to the enormous influx of people by selling goods and services like picks, shovels, blankets, and tents.

The anecdote I alluded to earlier in this chapter concerns the recent pandemic and the opportunity I saw in buying both Prudential and Metropolitan Life Insurance companies.

Unfortunately, millions of people died worldwide due to COVID-19. As a result, most life insurance companies' share prices declined precipitously because of the enormous number of death claims they had to pay out.

In my opinion, the stock market grossly overreacted. How?

PRU and Met's share prices declined by half in 2020. Yet, each only had about 6% of the U.S. market share, which translated into about 60,000 death claims—not millions, as Wall Street anticipated.

But here's what they forgot to consider: in 2021, the number of new life insurance policies sold saw its biggest increase in 50 years. In total, 43.1 million life insurance policies were purchased by Americans. 6% of 43 million is a lot of new business, revenue, and profits for PRU and MET!

The net result: both stocks doubled in just two years while paying a hefty dividend to yours truly. Any idea how happy I was with the outcome?

I highly recommend second-level thinking. Start by praying for original thoughts and ideas, wisdom, favor, insight, razor-sharp vision, and acute discernment. Remember, you have not because you ask not.

Meanwhile, back at the ranch, a final thought or two. If you invest in the stock market, do so for the long haul. Avoid short-term speculation; it's called gambling.

Never forget that the stock market giveth and the stock market taketh away. You must be diligent about keeping a close watch on your holdings.

I am often asked for investment tips in social settings. Folks want the next hot stock or a quick way to make a lot of money. Since I know my predicting powers are limited, I always suggest they purchase Irish stocks. "Irish stocks?" they respond in astonishment. "Why Irish stocks?" My answer is simple: "It's the only place on planet Earth where the capitol is Dublin!" Sorry, I couldn't resist.

All kidding aside, I have been to Ireland. It's a beautiful country; the lush, green, rolling hillsides dotted with sheep are breathtaking. Sheep are everywhere. It is estimated that Ireland has 3.5 million sheep. Of course, nobody knows for sure since whenever someone tries to count them, they fall asleep.[19] OK, OK. I can't help myself. *A merry heart does good, like medicine.* King Solomon, the wisest man who ever lived, said that. Who am I to disagree?

Enough nonsense; it is time to move on. But before I do, I want to share a story from the Bible that illustrates that our God is in the multiplication business.

The story is from Matthew 14:13-21 (NIV):

> [13]When Jesus heard what had happened, he withdrew by boat privately to a solitary place. Hearing of this, the crowds followed him on foot from the towns. [14]When Jesus landed and saw a large crowd, he had compassion on them and healed their sick. [15]As evening approached, the disciples came to him and said, "This is a remote place, and it's already getting late. Send the crowds away so they can go to the villages and buy themselves some food." [16]Jesus replied, "They do not need to go away. You give them something to eat." [17]"We have here only five loaves of bread and two fish," they answered. [18]"Bring them here to me," he said. [19]And he directed the people to sit down on the grass. Taking the five loaves and the two fish and looking up to heaven, he gave thanks and broke the loaves. Then he gave them to the disciples, and the disciples gave them to the people. [20]They all ate and were satisfied, and the disciples picked up twelve basketfuls of broken pieces

---

19 Ever wonder where the phrase "sis boom bah" came from? It's the last sound a sheep makes before it explodes ☺. Courtesy of Johnny Carson.

that were left over. [21]The number of those who ate was about five thousand men, besides women and children.

And who said there's no such thing as a free lunch? If Jesus can multiply five loaves and two fish, he can certainly multiply what you have. Be Blessed!

3.
LET'S DO SOME BONDING

Bonds have been called the stepchild of investments. However, they serve a useful purpose for many people (particularly income seekers).

I do have to confess, bonds are not flashy financial instruments, but they are necessary for a well-balanced portfolio. Almost all diversified portfolios contain a percentage in bonds.

What kind should you own?

To answer this question and clear up some costly misconceptions about bonds, you will need to read this short chapter. As I am faced with the daunting task of trying to make bonds interesting, I am reminded that my great-grandmother made me take a spoonful of castor oil daily when I was growing up because it was good for me. You should also read the next few pages for your own good!

In plain English, bonds are a loan between the bond issuer (a company or government) and an investor. The issuer is obligated to pay a specific amount of money (interest) over a specific period of time, often referred to as the bond's duration. An example will help:

Suppose the Ford Motor Company wants to build a new factory and assembly line to reintroduce the Edsel. Let's say that the estimated cost to build the new facility is $100 million. Where can the bigwigs at Ford go to raise the necessary funds for their newest brainchild?

What is a Bond?

According to *Investopedia*, a bond is a fixed-income investment in which an investor loans money to an entity (typically corporate or governmental) that borrows the funds for a defined period at a variable or fixed interest rate. Bonds are used by companies, municipalities, states, and sovereign governments to raise money and finance various projects and activities. Bond owners are the debtholders (or creditors) of the issuer.

A bank? Maybe, but that depends on many factors: interest rates, the financial condition of the banks, and the overall economy. Ford could also issue $100 million in new corporate bonds. Let's say that Ford hires an investment banker as an intermediary between itself and folks interested in buying bonds. Ford is now legally obliged to pay the agreed-upon interest rate (coupon) to the bond purchaser (you, the investor) for a fixed period (typically anywhere from three to ten years). Upon maturity, bondholders get their initial investment back as long as they keep their fingers crossed.

Here are a few basics:

1. Bonds are usually sold in $1,000 increments (or face value).
2. Bonds pay coupon (periodic interest) payments twice a year (typically at a fixed rate).

3. Bonds have a maturity date on which interest payments cease and your principal is repaid to you.

It is crucial to understand the difference between the various bond types since they are not all created equal. By doing so, you'll be able to make wiser investment decisions.

Let's begin by examining United States government marketable securities:

Treasury Bills. Mature in one year or less and pay a low interest rate.

Treasury Notes. Mature after one to ten years and pay a respectable rate of return.

Treasury Bonds. Maturities range from 20 to 30 years. These generally have a higher yield. Imagine buying a 30-year Treasury Bond yielding 13.45% in 1981. That's one I missed.

Treasury Inflation-Protected Securities (TIPS). Like treasuries, TIPS are backed by the federal government. Upon maturity, an investor can be certain of getting their principal back, plus a guaranteed fixed rate of return and a buffer against inflation! If the fixed interest rate falls short of inflation (as measured by the consumer price index), Uncle Sam pays a bonus to bridge the gap. Investors in TIPS are guaranteed to always keep pace with inflation. That's a good deal! Tips can be very useful during high inflationary times (like in 2022 when the CPI rose by 6.5 percent).

The four US Government securities are perceived to be the safest investments on Planet Earth (at least for now).

Municipal Bonds, a.k.a. Munis. These bonds are issued by state and local governments. Munis have favorable tax advantages for investors. Some are tax-free, depending on where you live. They are not as safe as U.S. Treasuries. However, munis carry very little default risk—except if you lived in Detroit in 2013 or Orange County, California, in 1994, when they filed for bankruptcy.

Corporate Bonds. Corporations raise funds for various capital projects (Ford Motor Company, for example) by issuing debt in the form of a corporate bond. Corporate bonds will (for the most part) pay a higher interest rate than U.S. Treasuries and munis. However, investors must deal with a higher risk of default.

Corporations can and do go out of business—think Enron, Lehman Brothers, and Silicon Valley Bank. Nevertheless, if you choose wisely, a corporate bond can be a rewarding fixed-income investment.

Caution: always check to see if the bond you're buying has a call feature. If so, the issuer has the right to redeem or pay you off prior to the bond's maturity date. I prefer to purchase bonds without a call provision because at least I know what I'm getting and for how long with no surprises. I hate surprises, and so should you. One way to determine if a bond is creditworthy is to check with the three major credit rating agencies: Moody's, S&P, and Fitch. Their job is to assign a credit rating to corporations issuing bonds. AAA indicates an "extremely strong" capacity to meet its financial commitments.

Quiz #1: What are the only two U.S. corporations with AAA ratings? (See the answer at the end of this chapter.)

BBB-rated bonds have an adequate capacity to meet their financial commitments. However, diverse or changing economic conditions could weaken a company's ability to meet its financial commitments.

CCC, or lower-rated bonds, have problems and are sometimes called 'junk bonds.' These are obviously risky, and unless you know what you are doing, you should avoid them. They are called 'junk' for very good reasons.

Beware, everyone makes mistakes—including the rating agencies. Enron was still rated investment grade four days before it declared bankruptcy. The big three rating agencies are still (to this day) criticized for failing to warn investors of the dangers of collateralized mortgage obligations (CMOs) securities during the 2008 financial crisis. Investors lost a bundle due to these guys' incompetence.

Speaking of CMOs, I'm reminded of a phone call I received from our bond desk back in 2007. The trader wanted to know why we weren't selling "very safe, high-yielding CMOs" to our clients. My response was simple: no matter how much research I did, I couldn't wrap my head around what was really going on. This 25-year-old "expert" offered to explain them to me, but after listening to him for about 15 minutes, I realized he didn't understand them either. Fortunately, I didn't sell a single CMO to my clients. Many CMOs ended up defaulting or downgrading to junk. Incidentally, if you are curious to know more about what went on behind the scenes of one of the biggest financial fiascoes in U.S. history, read *The Big Short* or watch the movie; both are quite entertaining. It will also give you a better idea of the kind of geniuses who run our financial system—very scary. The movie wasn't labeled H for Horror, but it should have been.

But back to bonds ...

Global Government Bonds. Another interesting option is global government bonds. They are issued and guaranteed by governments or authorities outside the United States. These bonds generally pay a higher yield than U.S. government bonds but have additional risks, such as political instability and currency fluctuations.

Zero-Coupon Bonds. These bonds pay no interest or coupon but are issued at a considerable discount to the face value. For example, you purchase a $1,000 bond for $500. You get $1,000 upon maturity—say in ten years. Think of a savings bond.

Convertible Bonds. This type of bond allows owners to convert their bonds into company stock at a predetermined price at a later date. They can be potentially very profitable if you know what you are doing.

For the most part, bonds are considered safer than stocks and generally have less volatility. If a corporation were to go out of business, a bondholder would have a higher claim to the remaining company assets than a stockholder. But you can still lose your shirt with bonds if you are not careful.

Here is the biggest takeaway from this chapter: bonds are interest-rate sensitive. If interest rates increase, bond values decrease, and vice versa. Think of a seesaw—when one side goes up, the other must go down.

An illustration is in order. If you bought a bond for $1,000 yielding 5% with a ten-year maturity, and interest rates rose to 6%, your bond would now be worth less if you wanted to sell it prior to maturity. Who would pay you the full price for your 5% bond when they could buy a 6% bond on the open market? You would have to discount your price to make your 5% bond attractive to a potential buyer. If, however, you held your 5% bond until maturity, you would receive your $1,000 face amount. Nevertheless, by doing so, you would miss out by not owning a 6% bond. *Comprendo? Capisce? Get it?* I hope so.

On the other hand, if interest rates decreased to 4%, your 5% bond would become more valuable. A person looking for higher yields (than 4%) would be willing to pay you a premium to get their hands on a 5% bond.

Take a deep breath; there is good news coming! The easy way to buy a diversified portfolio of bonds is by purchasing a bond mutual fund or exchange-traded fund (ETF), which we will explore in the next chapter.

Two vital questions must be addressed before we conclude this (most entertaining) chapter:

First, who should own a bond? Most people should consider owning them. Bonds provide relatively safe and predictable income. They are also a critical part of asset allocation, diversification, and risk mitigation (which we will discuss in greater detail in Chapter 7).

When is a good time to buy bonds? Generally, the answer is when interest rates are decreasing because your bond will likely increase in value. Avoid buying bonds in a rising interest rate environment because the price you pay for your bond will likely decrease and you will lose principal unless you hold it to maturity.

It is important to note that although U.S. stocks have generally outperformed all other U.S. investment classes,[20] in the long run, bonds outperformed stocks in the 1930s and 2000s.

It is also vital to remember that in the long run, we all die. Most investors I know don't give a hoot what happened 50, 70, or 100 years ago. It has absolutely no impact on our portfolios today. The point is that bonds sometimes give you a better return than stocks do—period. In fact, bonds outperformed stocks in ten of the 38 years from 1980 to 2017— about one out of every four years. Why is that important? It shows the value of asset allocation and the importance of a broadly diversified

---

20 According to Ibbotson SBBI® Yearbook, since the 1920s

portfolio. The bottom line? Bonds can be a safe haven sometimes and not so much at other times.

Here is a simple test. Which would you rather have owned in 2008? Barclay's aggregate bond index (which was up 5.24%) or the S&P 500 Index (which was down 37%)? If you chose the latter option, you would have to make 59% back just to break even ($100,000 – 37% = $63,000 / $63,000 x 59% = $100,170), which could take you a very long time. If, on the other hand, you chose Door #1 (bonds), you have the potential to become a great investor. Congratulations!

Before we move on to the next chapter, here's another story from the Bible that confirms our God is in the multiplication business:

> Then, when Job prayed for his friends, the Lord restored his wealth and happiness! In fact, the Lord gave him twice as much as before!
> — Job 42:10 (TLB)

QUIZ #1: Answer from page 55: Johnson and Johnson and Microsoft are the only two AAA-rated corporate bonds in America.

QUIZ #2: What is the biggest difference between a bond and a man? Answer: Bonds eventually mature!

4.
MUTUAL FUNDS AND EXCHANGE-TRADED FUNDS

The beauty of owning a mutual fund (MF) is instant diversification. The ugliness of owning one can be its extraordinarily high fees. Some funds charge as much as 3% or more per year.

The mutual fund industry has been around for a long time. The first modern-day fund started in 1924. The industry has grown substantially over the past several years. It is estimated there are around 8,000 MFs in the United States with assets worth approximately $20 trillion. That is an awful lot of money. MFs are managed investment funds that pool money from many investors to buy and sell securities in real estate, stocks, and bonds.

An MF's combined holdings are known as its portfolio. Investors buy into a MF by purchasing shares. Each share represents your proportional ownership in the fund. By owning shares, you now participate in the gains and losses the fund generates. Got it?

MFs make money in three ways:

1. From income earned through stock dividends and bond interest: a fund pays out nearly all its net income (after fees) over the course of a calendar year to the fund owners via quarterly or annual distributions.
2. Through capital gains: if a fund sells a security for more than its original purchase price, it is called a capital gain. Almost all MFs pass these gains on to their shareholders at the end of the year.
3. From capital appreciation: if a managed investment fund's holdings increase in price but are not sold by the fund manager, the MF's share price will also increase in value.

You can sell your MF shares any day the stock market is open to harvest your profits or limit your losses.

Some of the other positive things MFs offer are:

Professional management: MF managers do a great deal of research before buying securities for their portfolios. They also monitor each holding in the fund and make decisions to sell. Their job is to stay on top of things and make adjustments as needed. Most of the larger MF companies have dozens of quants (quantitative analysts) scurrying about giving recommendations and advice to the various portfolio managers.

Another advantage MFs offer is **affordability**. Most funds have a relatively low dollar amount for initial and subsequent investment purchases. Some MFs allow you to start investing with as little as $25 to $50 per month if you set up an electronic funds transfer (EFT) through your checking or savings account. By far, **diversification** is a managed investment fund's best attribute. MFs must invest in an array of holdings. By doing so, they spread out the risk over dozens, if not hundreds, of stocks and/or bonds. MFs also offer **liquidity**. An investor in MFs can easily sell their shares for whatever the current value is at the end of any trading day.

And finally, it is easy to track and monitor your MF. You can look up your fund's performance, pricing, and value on the mutual fund's company website 24/7.

A quick overview of the basic types of mutual funds:

Stock or equity funds. A stock fund will generally invest at least 80% of its assets in common stocks of companies the managers expect to appreciate in value over time or in dividend-paying stocks.

Bond funds. Obviously, bond MFs invest in bonds and other debt securities. However, you need to know that there are several types of bond funds, i.e., corporate, government, municipal, etc. All bond funds are not created equal, nor do they perform the same. I suggest you review the bond chapter before purchasing a bond fund.

Balanced funds. A balanced fund will buy both stocks and bonds. A word of caution: these mutual funds can and will differ in their allocations. For instance, some will apportion 70% stocks to 30% bonds, most will have a 60% stock to 40% bond split, and some will allocate 50% to stocks and 50% to bonds. You should know how the fund is allocated before you invest. The higher the percentage in stocks, the more volatility you may have to put up with.

Global funds. Simply put, global funds will invest in equities from most of the developed countries around the world, including the U.S.. Buyer beware: I have seen some global funds with 80% of their stock holdings in U.S. companies—that may not get you the diversification you desire.

International funds. Exclude U.S. stocks and only invest abroad.

Sector funds. These funds invest in a specific industry of the economy, for instance, healthcare, technology, or the financial arena. Investors who work in these fields may see growth potential. Sector funds enable these folks to invest in what they know best.

Index funds. Index funds attempt to match or track the components of a market index, such as the S&P 500, a small-cap index, or a mid-cap index. An index fund is designed to provide broad market exposure, low expenses, and low portfolio turnover, thus reducing taxes and trading costs.

By no means are mutual funds the perfect investment. They have disadvantages. Some of these flaws can cost a small fortune. In my opinion, the biggest drawback is the fees they charge.

> In the short term, the impact of costs may appear modest, but over the long run, investment costs become immensely damaging to an investor's standard of living. Think long-term!
>
> — JOHN BOGLE,
> FOUNDER OF THE VANGUARD GROUP

Depending on what research you rely on, the average cost to own an actively managed fund is around 2 to 2.5% per year. That is an average, meaning that many funds charge much more.

All mutual funds charge an expense ratio, which represents a percentage of the assets they manage. After all, everyone needs to get paid. The average portfolio manager makes a little less than $500k per year. *You* help pay their mortgage and Porsche payments. There are also transaction costs since managers buy and sell securities regularly. Some funds have 100% turnover[21] or more during a single year. That is a lot of trading, and guess who pays for the trading costs? You do.

You may also pay sales charges and other fees. People who sell you these investments also need to get paid. According to the *Investment Company Institute Fact Book,*[22] the average sales charge for stock funds was 5.4%, and the average for bond funds was 3.9%. Believe it or not, another fee some MF companies charge is called a 12b-1. That is to cover advertising and marketing expenses. Isn't that nice of them?

Over the years, I have had several potential clients come to see me for advice or a second opinion on their investment portfolios. I can't tell you how often these folks had no idea how many fees they were paying to their fund company. Some even insisted they were not paying any fees. My question to them was: "Who works for free?"

Most of the disclosures about costs and fees are buried in the prospectus, which virtually no one reads—except me. The regulators (in their infinite wisdom) think it is in the investor's best interest to have their MF company print a 200-page document written in legalese that no one understands except those with a law degree. You pretty much need a Ph.D. in cryptography to fully understand a prospectus or be the kind of person who enjoys having a root canal done without anesthesia. The fees are there, but good luck trying to find them! Finally, you pay the MF company a maintenance fee for the privilege of letting them maintain your retirement account and send you quarterly statements. Of course, if you want to save the planet (who wouldn't?), the MF company

---

21 Portfolio turnover is a measure of how frequently assets within a fund are bought and sold over the course of a year.

22 2011 edition

will allow you to download your statement instead of mailing it to you. Same fee, but the earth is a better place to live, and the MF industry keeps getting richer.

So, let's bottom line it. If you add up the fees, charges, and cash drag,[23] you are at around 2.27%, plus any initial sales charges you paid (give or take a few basis points). What does that mean for the average investor? If your fund had a gross return for the year of 10%, you would net 7.73% after deductions. If you paid a sales charge or load of, say, 5% on an initial $10,000 investment, you would receive a 7.73% return on $9,500 (or $734).

Think about that for a minute. You put up 100% of the initial investment capital and assume 100% of the market risk, but you only receive a fraction of the gains. Oh, and by the way, they get their 2.27% even if your MF had a down year. How does that work? If the gross return is minus 10%, your account will decline by 12.27%. They still need to get paid for the fine job they did or didn't do. Lovely, isn't it?

Now ponder this: the difference between paying 1%[24] in annual fees versus 2% on a $100,000 investment over a 30-year period can cost you about $200,000. I hope you grasp the importance of low fees. $200k is a lot of money. High fees can severely damage your economic well-being.

Are you beginning to see that MFs have a parasitic nature? Next, let's talk taxes.

Long-term capital gains and dividends are normally taxed at lower rates than ordinary income tax rates. Short-term capital gains (shares held for one year or less), however, are generally taxed at ordinary income

---

23 MFs must keep a portion of their assets in cash (around 2 to 5%) for new purchases and redemptions. The interest rate on cash is generally close to nothing, thus lowering portfolio returns because they are not 100% invested.

24 I'll show you how to lower your fees to 1% later in the book.

tax rates. Why is that important? A Morningstar analyst estimated the average turnover ratio (explained earlier) for a managed domestic stock fund was 130%, creating a great deal of short-term capital gains, which are almost always taxed at a higher rate.

Another enormous problem with mutual funds is underperformance. Roughly 90% of all actively managed funds failed to beat the S&P 500 Index over a 15-year period. That being the case, most investors are grossly overpaying for mediocre returns. Based on the evidence, investors should seriously consider stacking the deck in their favor by investing in an index fund that tracks the S&P 500.

> It has been shown that active managers are not able to outperform sufficiently to offset the costs that they impose on investors.
>
> — JEREMY SIEGEL, AUTHOR OF
> STOCKS FOR THE LONG RUN

Another factor to consider? According to the American Association of Individual Investors, only 6.85% of solo MF managers last ten years in their roles. Morningstar states that 34% of all managers change jobs in just one year alone. That can be very problematic. Suppose you do your research and find a MF you really like. It has an excellent long-term track record with lower-than-average fees. You buy the fund, only to find out a year later that your fund manager moved on to greener pastures. Needless to say, the MF company doesn't make a big deal about it; they don't want their investors to make a mass exodus. So, what do you do? It depends. Does the new manager have an excellent track record, or is it some clueless guy or gal straight out of business school with no practical experience?

You may want to consider transferring your account to where your old manager ended up. Sometimes, it makes more sense to buy the manager and not the fund; sometimes it doesn't.

Either way, do your homework before you decide.

One final point: according to Morningstar, nearly half of U.S. stock funds report no manager ownership. In other words, about 50% of these professional money managers don't invest their own money in the funds they run. That is certainly worth sustained reflection, don't you think? I can't fathom why anyone would invest in a fund that its manager doesn't invest in. You would think an ethical manager would want to show they believe in their fund and are willing to pay the same costs and taxes their shareholders pay. I don't think you would see this kind of behavior in a monastery. I also don't think you will disagree with me—manager ownership is a clear signal of commitment (or lack thereof) and faith in the funds they manage. If the most reliable advocate for a product or service is its user, and only about 50% of portfolio managers invest their own money in the funds they manage, what does that say to you? It speaks volumes to me.

Next, let's talk about the ABCs of mutual fund share classes. Many MF companies offer more than one class of shares to investors. Each class represents a similar interest in the portfolio. However, the primary difference between the classes is the fees you are charged.

For example, **Class A shares** have a front-end sales charge, usually 4 to 5%. If you invest $10,000, you pay $400 to $500 upfront (which is deducted from your original $10k), plus an ongoing annual management fee. However, the more you invest, the lower the initial sales charge. For example, you may only pay 2 to 3% upfront on a $100,000 investment.

Class B shares do not charge a front-end commission, but they charge a contingent deferred sales charge if you sell your shares within a certain period (usually five to six years). The good news is that all your initial investment goes to work for you right away. The bad news is you will generally pay higher internal expenses.

Class C shares don't impose a front-end sales charge if you hold your shares for at least a year. You won't pay a contingent deferred sales charge after the first year or two, but the internal fees, in most cases, are higher than class A and B shares.

No-load funds are purchased without commission or a sales charge. You can buy no-load funds directly from the investment company, not a broker or salesperson. The reason a salesperson (who is commission-driven) will not recommend a no-load fund is that they don't get paid for doing so. There is nothing in it for them.

Finally, there are **institutional shares**. These shares are generally only available to large investors or institutions like pension funds. The minimum investment is anywhere from $100,000 to $25,000,000. However, smaller investors can gain access to these attractive shares through a Registered Investment Advisor (RIA). We will talk more about them later.

The primary advantage of institutional shares is lower expense ratios, which translates into higher returns for the investor.

Some final words of caution:

I have met too many people who chase the latest hot mutual fund. Just because a fund was a top performer last year doesn't mean it will be this year.

I am reminded of a story that illustrates the point.

Bruce was one of our new financial planners several years back. A Yale graduate, he was very bright—so smart that he aced the Series 7 securities test (a very difficult exam with only a 65% pass rate) before coming to work for us. One morning, Bruce came into my office with his newspaper in hand, wanting to know if I had read the financial section. He enthusiastically wanted me to know that the Russia fund was the top-performing MF for the past quarter. "Shouldn't we be putting some of our clients' money in the top-performing fund?" he asked. With my less-than-excitable British demeanor, I told him to hold on to the newspaper for three months and then ask me the same question. I informed him the Russia fund would probably end up on the worst-performing MF list for the next calendar quarter. Sure enough, he walked into my office 91 days later and asked, "How did you know that would happen?" The Russia fund was indeed the worst-performing mutual fund for the past quarter. I attribute my predicting powers more to common sense than my crystal ball. When any investment becomes overpriced (hot), it is bound to fall—usually sooner rather than later. You really need to be careful when buying red-hot mutual funds.

A couple of final thoughts before we move on to exchange-traded funds (ETFs):

No one is perfect; everyone has down years. For example, Bill Miller (one of the most successful mutual fund managers in history) beat the S&P 500 Index for 15 straight years, from 1991 to 2005 (a remarkable feat), only to lose the entire 15-year gain in just two years, 2007 and 2009. My point is that no one can constantly perform well. Sooner or later, they will have a bad year. Or, as Yogi Berra so astutely said, "Every Napoleon meets his Waterloo."

Let's be absolutely clear. No one (and I mean no one) can identify next year's top-performing mutual fund or portfolio manager in advance. Avoid those who claim they can.

Case in point: over 1,000 mutual funds owned Enron stock when it went down like the *Titanic*. That's about one out of four equity fund managers caught asleep at the helm.

Are **exchange-traded funds** a better choice than mutual funds? Let's take a closer look. Exchange-traded funds (ETFs) are pools of money that track indexes like the S&P 500, NASDAQ 100, or Russell 2000. When you buy shares of an ETF, you buy shares of a diversified portfolio that tracks the total overall return of its index.

ETFs are traded like stocks on all three major stock exchanges. You can trade an ETF any time the stock markets are open, and you can do so in real-time. A mutual fund, on the other hand, gets bought or sold at the close of business each trading day. Why might that be important? Suppose we encounter another 9/11 event. Would you want to sell your investments (or have your Registered Investment Advisor sell them for you) immediately or at the end of the trading day after a severe market decline?

The ETF industry started 25 years ago. ETFs have since become one of the most popular investment vehicles, boasting over one trillion dollars under management.

Like mutual funds, there are various types of exchange-traded funds. You can choose a stock, bond, international, or sector ETF.

The beauty of ETFs is that they have far more benefits than MFs—for instance, **tax efficiency.** According to Fidelity.com, ETFs have two major tax advantages compared to mutual funds. Due to structural differences, mutual funds typically incur more capital gains taxes than ETFs. Moreover, capital gains tax on an ETF is incurred only upon the sale of the ETF by the investor, whereas mutual funds pass on capital gains taxes to investors through the life of the investment.

In short, ETFs have lower capital gains and are payable only upon the sale of the ETF.

Capital gains that get passed on to the investor in a typical stock mutual fund can be between 5 to 6% annually versus less than 1% in an ETF. Another benefit is **cost efficiency**. Because an ETF tracks an index and is not actively managed like most mutual funds, ETF fees can be substantially lower. There is no manager to pay, no commissions or front-end loads to pay, and with virtually no trading costs, your annual savings is around 0.75% to 1%.

I cannot overemphasize how vital 1% annually is to your financial well-being over the long term. You waste tens of thousands of dollars in a $100,000 portfolio and hundreds of thousands in a million-dollar nest egg over an investing lifetime! Exchange-traded funds are not for everyone, however. They do have some challenges if you want to set up a periodic investment plan with small dollar amounts.

Okay, let's recap. Why an exchange-traded fund instead of a mutual fund?

Fees matter. So do taxes, trading costs, and commissions.

Most knowledgeable investors agree the pluses of ETFs overshadow those of a managed investment fund by a sizable margin. To be a great investor, you must invest wisely. A wise investor keeps their eyes on fees, charges, and expenses. Focus on what matters.

Here is another story from the Bible that illustrates how our God is in the multiplication business:

The miraculous catch of fish!

[1]On one occasion, while the crowd was pressing in on him to hear the word of God, he was standing by the lake of Gennesaret, [2]and he saw two boats by the lake, but the fishermen had gone out of them and were washing their nets. [3]Getting into one of the boats, which was Simon's, he asked him to put out a little from the land. And he sat down and taught the people from the

boat. ⁴And when he had finished speaking, he said to Simon, "Put out into the deep and let down your nets for a catch." ⁵And Simon answered, "Master, we toiled all night and took nothing! But at your word, I will let down the nets." ⁶And when they had done this, they enclosed a large number of fish, and their nets were breaking. ⁷They signaled to their partners in the other boat to come and help them. And they came and filled both the boats, so that they began to sink. ⁸But when Simon Peter saw it, he fell down at Jesus' knees, saying, "Depart from me, for I am a sinful man, O Lord." ⁹For he and all who were with him were astonished at the catch of fish that they had taken.

— Luke 5:1-9 (ESV)

If God can multiply fish, He can certainly multiply what you have.

P.S. I received some very good news while I was writing this chapter. My wife's credit card was stolen. Why is that good news? So far, whoever has it is spending less than my wife!

5.
REAL ESTATE INVESTMENT TRUSTS

For years, real estate investment trusts (REITs) have been an excellent investment to own in a diversified portfolio. A REIT is a professionally managed company that owns or finances income-producing real estate. REITs can provide investors with regular income streams, capital appreciation, and diversification.

Unlike other investments, REITs must pay out at least 90% of their taxable income as dividends to shareholders. As you may recall from an earlier chapter, dividends are generally taxed at a lower rate than ordinary income. That's a good thing. Publicly traded REITs are bought and sold on the major stock exchanges like individual stocks, making them extremely liquid and desirable. Real estate investment trusts were created by Congress[25] (the opposite of progress) and signed into law by President Dwight D. Eisenhower in 1960. Since then, the REIT industry has grown into a trillion-dollar business.

---

25 The proper collective noun for a group of baboons—honest.

More importantly, REITs have historically been one of the better-performing asset classes, outperforming bonds and commodities. REITs are tied to almost all aspects of the U.S. economy, including apartments,[26] hospitals, hotels, office buildings, nursing homes, shopping malls, and storage centers.

They exist in all 50 states and over 30 countries. Conceptually, this is how a REIT works (take Walmart, CVS, or Costco, for example). Suppose they want to open a new location. Instead of spending millions of their own dollars and valuable human resources, they partner with a real estate investment trust. The REIT raises money from thousands of investors like you and me. The REIT builds the store and leases it back to the retailer. It's a win-win business transaction for everyone. CVS gets to open a new pharmacy for relatively little capital outlay (they don't have to tie up millions of dollars to build a new drugstore). The REIT makes money by collecting rent payments from CVS, and investors (us) get a monthly or quarterly dividend, combined with long-term appreciation as the share price increases. REITs have provided investors with very attractive total return performance over the years.

I have personally found REITs an efficient way to diversify my portfolio. By investing in a REIT, I can own a part of a 7-Eleven in New York, a Taco Bell in Texas, and an L.A. Fitness Center in California, all in a single investment. Or I can own a piece of the Empire State Building in an office REIT.

Real estate investment trusts are a passive investor's dream come true—no toilets to fix, no repairs to make, no tenants to chase for rent payments, and no destructive renters to clean up after.

Here are some pros and cons of the main types of publicly traded REITs:

---

26 I'm not sure why they call them apartments since they are all connected.

Retail REITs. Approximately 24% of REIT investments are in shopping malls and freestanding retail, representing the single biggest investment by type in America. Whatever shopping center you frequent is likely owned by a REIT. Before investing in retail real estate, one should examine the retail industry. Is it financially healthy, and what is the outlook for the future? It's crucial to remember that retail REITs make money from the rent they charge tenants. If retailers experience cash flow problems due to poor sales, they could delay or default on those monthly payments or, even worse, file for bankruptcy. At that point, a new tenant must be found, which can be challenging in difficult economic times. Therefore, it is crucial that you invest in REITs with the strongest anchor tenants possible, including grocery, home improvement stores and warehouse clubs.

Residential REITs. These REITs own and operate multifamily rental properties, apartment buildings, and manufactured housing. When looking to invest in this type of REIT, one should consider several factors before jumping in. For instance, the best apartment markets tend to be where homes are very expensive relative to the rest of the country. In places like New York, Chicago, and Los Angeles, the high cost of single-family homes forces more people to rent, which drives up the price landlords can charge each month. As a result, the biggest residential REITs tend to focus on large urban centers.

Healthcare REITs. Healthcare REITs will be an increasing subsector to watch as Americans age and healthcare costs continue to climb. Healthcare REITs invest in the real estate of hospitals, medical centers, nursing facilities, and retirement homes. The success of this kind of real estate is directly tied to the healthcare system. Most of the operators of these facilities rely on occupancy fees, Medicare and Medicaid reimbursements, and private pay. If you are sick and tired of paying high medical expenses, consider owning healthcare REITs. By doing so, you get a piece of the action. A side note: since hospitals, nursing homes, and doctors rarely move because of the high cost of relocating, healthcare REITs are relatively safe with very predictable income.

Office REITs. Office REITs invest in office buildings. They receive rental income from tenants, who usually sign long-term leases. These properties can range from skyscrapers to office parks. Some focus on central business districts or suburban areas; others emphasize specific tenants such as government agencies. The thing to know about these REITs is when our country goes through a recession, vacancies increase. The flip side is when our economy is doing well, occupancies increase, and so does the rent. That is good news for you.

Mortgage REITs. Approximately 10% of REIT investments are in mortgages rather than real estate. The best known (but not necessarily the best investments) are Fannie Mae and Freddie Mac, government-sponsored enterprises that buy mortgages in the secondary market. Some mortgage REITs are highly leveraged (debt), which can work in your favor, or not. They can also be volatile with interest rate swings. Be careful and be sure you know what you are buying.

Data Center REITs. Data Center REITs are a relatively new form of REIT. The need for data storage (the cloud) has grown substantially over the past ten years. Simply put, data center REITs own and manage facilities their customers use to store data safely. Think about all the information Facebook, Google, and Amazon must store in a secure facility. The future of data storage looks promising.

One last example before moving on:

Lodging REITs. Lodging REITs own and manage hotels and resorts throughout the world. In turn, guests (business travelers and vacationers) get to "rent" a room for $50 to $500 per night. Think about a hotel "renting" the same room for $100 per night for 300 nights out of every year. That is $30,000! Not bad for an average-size room of just over 300 square feet. Marriott, Hilton, and the Sheraton hotel chains use REITs to grow their business. Of course, the biggest downside would be if people stopped traveling due to another 9/11-type event or pandemic. If that were to happen, most of us would feel far more comfortable in our own homes until the dust settled.

There is also a second class of REITs called nonlisted or nontraded real estate investment trusts. They are registered with the Securities and Exchange Commission and are required to distribute most of their taxable income to shareholders, like publicly traded REITs. However, they are illiquid (they cannot be easily sold). Your money could be tied up for three to five years or longer. Despite this negative feature, they are worth looking at for investors with long-term time horizons.

A few years back, I invested in a nonlisted REIT. I received a 7% dividend for about three to four years until it went public by issuing an IPO. The share price jumped by 40% in the first two trading days. On a scale of one to ten, I would say that was awesome!

Of course, I was deliriously happy in a British sort of way. These deals don't always turn out this well, but some do and are worth considering. Eventually, non-listed REITs will either go public or sell their real estate holdings and distribute the proceeds to their shareholders. Sometimes they sell all of their holdings as a package to a large institutional investor such as a pension or endowment fund.

Let's wrap it up. REITs offer investors several benefits, including:

1. Diversification: Over the long term, equity REIT returns have shown little correlation to the returns of the broader stock market.
2. Dividends: Stock exchange-listed REITs have provided a stable income stream to investors.
3. Liquidity: Stock exchange-listed REIT shares can be easily bought and sold.
4. Performance: Over the past 20 years (ending in 2021), most stock exchange-listed REIT returns have outperformed the S&P 500, Dow Jones Industrials, and NASDAQ Composite.
5. Transparency: Stock exchange-listed REITs operate under the same rules as other public companies for securities, regulatory and financial reporting purposes.

Never forget that all investments have some risk, including real estate investment trusts. Poor management, vacancies, business failures, and overpaying for your shares—especially overpaying—will jeopardize your long-term investment returns. Always do your homework before investing!

Or, as the Bible warns...

My people are destroyed for lack of knowledge.
— HOSEA 4:6 (NKJV)

Here's a great example from the Bible that dramatically illustrates multiplication:

> In those days, Peter stood up among the believers (a group numbering about a hundred and twenty).
> **ACTS 1:15 (NIV)**

> Those who accepted his message were baptized, and about three thousand were added to their number that day.
> **ACTS 2:41 (NIV)**

In a single day, 3,000 new believers were added to the "church." That's a 2,500% increase, and that's awesome!

I am reminded of a true story relating to real estate as I close this chapter. My wife and I were building a house several years ago (I had retired, and we wanted to downsize). When we gave our wish list to our builder, he came back to us with a higher price than we were willing to pay. So, the three of us talked it over. We went from a three-car garage to a two and cut the room sizes, but we were still over budget. Finally, in frustration, I said to my wife: "Why don't we eliminate the kitchen since you no longer cook?"

Yes, we are still married!

6.
ANNUITIES

What do Beethoven, Ben Franklin, and Babe Ruth have in common (besides being old, famous, dead guys)? These three distinguished gentlemen owned annuities.

When Ruth retired in 1935, at the height of the Great Depression, he and his wife lived comfortably on the monthly payments from his annuities.[27]

Ben Franklin, one of our nation's Founding Fathers and the face on our one-hundred-dollar bill, gave Boston and Philadelphia annuities in his will. Historians say the $4,400 annuity for Boston grew to $5.5 million. After paying the city income for more than 200 years, the short-sighted politicians in Beantown decided to close the account and cash out.[28]

Beethoven (best known for decomposing after his death) was given a very generous annuity over 200 years ago to motivate him to stay in Vienna to compose and perform his music.

---

27 Source: Irene Jarosewich: "Insurance Matters"

28 Source: The Center for Annuity Awareness

Annuities have been around for a very long time. In fact, the idea of paying out a stream of income to a family or individual dates back to the Roman Empire.

So, what exactly is an annuity?

An annuity is a policy or savings plan (issued by an insurance company) designed to accept and grow funds on a tax-deferred basis. Annuities can also create an income stream for a fixed number of years or for a lifetime. The money deposited into an annuity can be a lump sum, regular periodic payments, or a combination of both. In simplistic terms, you give the insurance company your money now and receive income from them at a later date.

There are two types of annuities: fixed and variable. In a variable annuity (VA), your principal value varies based on the performance of the subaccounts in which you choose to invest your money.

Subaccounts are managed by a specialist or team of specialists who make buy-and-sell decisions based on the subaccount's investment objective. Much like a mutual fund, subaccounts come in all sizes and flavors. You can invest in an aggressive growth account or a global, bond, balanced, gold, utility, etc. account.

Two of a VA's key features are the guaranteed minimum death benefit (GMDB) and the annuity income rider. The GMDB is generally equal to the total amount of money you invested into your account minus any prior withdrawals (no matter how poorly your account did) or your contract value at death—whichever is greater.

Say you invest $100,000 in a VA and experience a decline of 20% in your subaccount. A year later, you die of a heart attack. Your beneficiary receives one hundred thousand dollars. If, on the other hand, your $100k grows to $200k over the next several years, and you pass away, your heirs get two hundred thousand dollars.

The annuity income rider provides a lifetime income stream and typically has a guaranteed growth rate. In other words, you pay an extra fee for the rider. In return, you receive regular increases in your monthly check over time for as long as you live, no matter how long you live. The annuity income rider helps solve the ever-growing problem of longevity risk we seniors face—as if living too long is a problem. I suppose it can be if we run out of money.

Who should consider owning a variable annuity? It depends. VAs are generally suitable for individuals who want upside potential in the stock market: people willing to put up with volatility who want a guarantee on their principal. VAs almost always have higher fees and expenses than fixed annuities, averaging around 2.5% annually.

While on the subject of fees, I feel compelled to make additional contemptuous remarks about financial journalists. It drives me nuts when these incompetent English majors with little or no financial backgrounds write articles that claim, "Annuities have high fees." I've read dozens of these masterpieces over my career. They all say basically the same thing, which leads me to believe they plagiarize each other's content. Ignorance must feel better when it is shared. Or, as the old Irish saying goes, experts are men who educate themselves by reading each other's work. I would encourage you to ignore those people behind the curtain. For the most part, they are guilty of *groupthink*. Few reporters do their own critical thinking. Many have not had an original thought since they discovered plagiarism.

For the heck of it, I googled "annuities have high fees." Google came up with 34,500,000 results. By just reading the first ten sources, you would swear they were written by the same person. These clueless reporters have no idea what they are talking about. What exactly do they mean when they say, "Annuities have high fees?" Are they referring to fixed, immediate, or fixed indexed annuities? Almost all these annuities have absolutely no fees unless you decide to add a rider.

These are the same geniuses who mocked the possibility of space travel.[29] Meanwhile, back on Planet Earth, these guys think that by setting the facts aside, they can draw whatever conclusions they want. The reality is most fixed annuities do not have fees—period. I realize I need to pick up the pace here. When dealing with annuities, it can sometimes feel like we are moving at a glacial speed. So, let's move on to fixed annuities.

There are four types:

1. **Immediate annuities** start paying an income stream in less than a year.
2. **Deferred annuities** start paying an income stream anywhere from one to 50 years.
3. **Multi-year guarantee annuities** pay a fixed interest rate each year for a certain period: one, five, or ten years.
4. **Fixed indexed annuities (FIAs)** increase in value depending on the performance of a baseline index like the S&P 500, Dow Jones, or FTSE[30].

Bias Alert!

There are two types of people in this world: those who know they are biased in some way, shape, or form and those who are in denial. I freely admit to my partisan stance on fixed indexed annuities (FIA). On a personal level, they have proven to be one of my best-performing investments over the past two decades. Here's why: FIAs are designed

---

29 Time Magazine 1920 editorial, later retracted on July 12, 1969, the day after Apollo II took off for the moon.

30 The Financial Times Stock Exchange 100 Index

to protect your retirement nest egg and savings. They are tax-deferred and structured to provide long-term income needs.

FIAs provide guarantees against the loss of principal and a guaranteed death benefit to a named beneficiary. With a fixed indexed annuity, you can participate in a market index like the S&P 500 and share in the gains in the up years but never incur a loss in the down years. I hope you grasp the significance of a product that allows you to make a percentage of the stock market gains but not the losses!

These guarantees are made by the insurance company issuing the annuity. So, only buy an annuity from a solid insurance company backed by the claims-paying ability of the best of the best.

> Social Security lasts for life, and so does an employer pension. If you don't have a pension, annuities can serve as a pension substitute.
>
> **— AARP**

Here's a great example of how an FIA can perform: my own fixed indexed annuity.

Yes, I eat my own cooking and put my money where my mouth is! Back in 2004, the stock market began to misbehave—again. I remember telling my wife we should start looking for a safer place to put some of our retirement funds. The volatility was like being on a roller-coaster ride. We decided to roll over one of our retirement accounts into an FIA. On August 17, 2004, we transferred $90,500. At the end of five years, on August 16, 2009, our balance was $127,996.71.

Was that good or bad? You can't tell unless you have something to compare it to. The S&P 500, for the same period, lost 8%. In other words, my $90,500 original deposit would have been worth only $83,000 (not counting any fees and commissions) if I had invested my money in an

S&P 500 Index fund. Focusing on the key numbers, my FIA account balance on August 16, 2009, was $127,996.71. If I had invested the same dollars in the S&P 500, my balance on August 16, 2009, would have been $83,260—almost a $45,000 difference! Sorry, but I must brag. That turned out to be a home run!

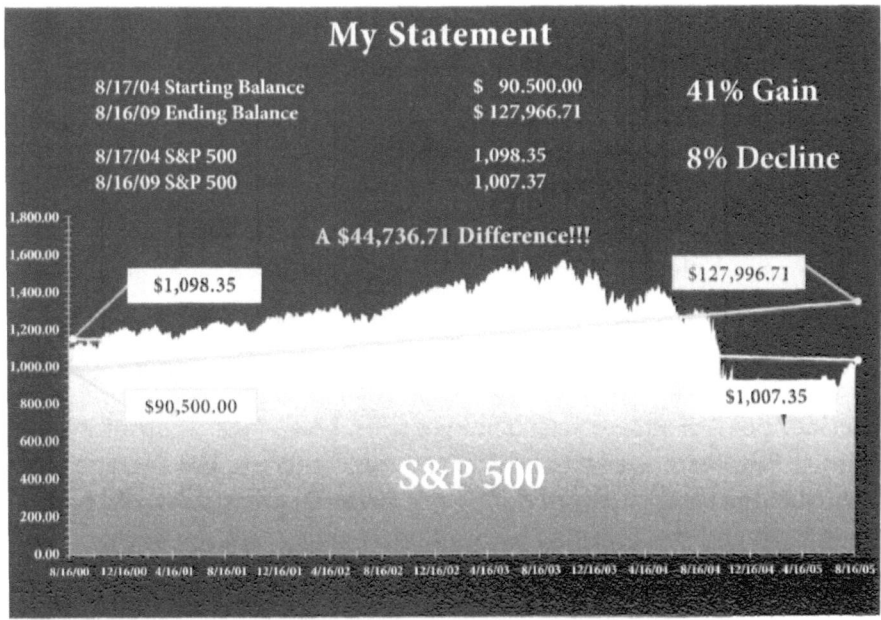

So, why do these FIAs do so well against the stock market and other investments? It's the value of zero. Remember, when the stock market has a down year, you don't lose money; you get zero. You have to admit that zero is better than a negative stock market return, not to mention peace of mind! FIAs prove their worth, especially in times of trouble. I think we can all agree that no one likes losing money.

In a hypothetical illustration done in July 2009 by Jack Marrion, president of Advantage Compendium (a St. Louis-based consulting firm), if FIAs were available back in the 1920s and '30s, the average annual index annuity return during the Great Depression would have been 6.4%, and this is during a decade that ended 65% lower than when it began. That is impressive —VERY impressive!

So, if you are concerned that you might have to go back to work when the stock market takes another hit, or if thinking about running out of money keeps you up at night, maybe a fixed index annuity is something you should consider. FIAs are designed to provide a guaranteed lifetime income. That sounds very attractive for anyone who might need to stretch retirement funds for 30 to 40 years! Don't take part in America's "retirement crisis." Instead, think about waking up in the morning knowing a check is coming soon. As Warren Buffett said a few years ago: "The two most beautiful words in the English language are, 'Check Enclosed.'"

Buffett also said that when it comes to investing, there are two main rules:

Rule #1: Never lose money. Rule #2: Never forget Rule #1.

> Who might want to buy an index annuity? Anyone who wants to invest in the market but is afraid of losing any money.
>
> — SUZE ORMAN, AUTHOR AND TV HOST

Should you consider owning an annuity? It depends. I don't think a 25-year-old should be looking to invest in an annuity. A 40-year-old might want to start thinking about it. There is no magic age. Annuities are long-term investments; you cannot access your funds until age 59½ without paying a penalty. I also think you shouldn't consider an annuity unless you have fully funded your other retirement plan options, such as a 401(k), Roth IRA, or SIMPLE plan. It should also depend on what you are trying to achieve: income, growth, or safety. These are my thoughts only. There is no definitive concrete answer as to who should (or should not) buy an annuity.

Remember, no single investment is perfect for everyone. Annuities make a lot of sense when diversification and safety are important to you. Make no mistake about it: annuities also have disadvantages. They are not FDIC-insured, even if you buy them at a bank. Don't be misled. I've come across several people who think that just because they have purchased financial products, including variable annuities, mutual funds, and fixed annuities from a bank, they are FDIC-insured. Not so!

Most annuities have surrender charges if you make withdrawals in the first five to ten years. Your friends at the IRS will penalize you 10% on withdrawals made prior to age 59½. It seems tax collectors are as busy today as they were in Jesus's day.

At this point, it might make sense to do a brief recap on fixed annuities. Your principal is fixed and guaranteed by the insurance company. Gains are usually locked in each year, and you can mix and match different types of annuities to create a guaranteed tax-favored[31] income stream in retirement that is not influenced by interest rates, market fluctuations, or other market influences.

Finally, what about the guy who promotes the "I Hate Annuities, and So Should You" ads? First, he was a financial columnist until a few years ago—STRIKE ONE. You already know how I feel about those people. Secondly, he told his readers in 2007, "The S&P 500 will be up in 2008" and "America should do well." Reality check: The S&P 500 was minus 37%, one of the worst declines in history—STRIKE TWO. Finally, his mutual fund performed so poorly that he was forced to close

---

31 Part of each payment is considered a return of capital on a non-qualified annuity and is, therefore, nontaxable. The formula for determining the nontaxable portion of each payment is determined in the IRS Code § 72(b)(1).

it in June of 2016. How bad was the performance? According to Fool. com, his fund wound up underperforming the S&P 500 Index by 21% over a three-year period and 52% over five years—STRIKE THREE. You're out! Case closed. This joker is nothing more than a shameless self-promoter. Stay away from him—and his advice. Always be careful who you listen to.

Go to my website, GreatInvestor.org, to download a copy of *Retirement Money Deserves a Good Home*. The free booklet offers strategies to get your money working harder and smarter.

OK, stick a fork in me—I'm done!

Here's another example from the Bible that illustrates how our God is in the multiplication business:

> So, Abram went up from Egypt to the Negev, with his wife and everything he had, and Lot went with him. Abram had become very wealthy in livestock and in silver and gold.
>
> — GENESIS 13:1-2 (NIV)

P.S. Sorry, but I can't resist:

A survey of graduating high school seniors revealed that more than 50% thought Sodom and Gomorrah were husband and wife—another glaring example of our tax dollars at work. Even grown-ups have trouble with history: At least 12% of American adults believe Joan of Arc was Noah's wife.

You can't make this stuff up.

7.

HOW TO CONSTRUCT A PORTFOLIO THAT IS RIGHT FOR YOU

R isk is inevitable. All investments have some level of risk. For instance, bonds have default and interest rate risk; foreign stocks have currency and political risks; REITs have vacancy risks. CDs, although relatively safe, aren't risk-free. Penalties for early withdrawal, inflation, and taxes can erode your savings rapidly. Companies go out of business or file for bankruptcy all the time: Lehman Brothers, General Motors, Toys "R" Us, and

Women and Investing

I recorded a podcast not too long ago called "Women and Investing." I would encourage the ladies reading this book to listen to it when you get a chance. It deals with the problems women face with the death of a spouse or divorce. You need to be aware of and involved in your family's financial decisions. Visit GreatInvestor.org. It's free and informative.

Enron, to name a few. Anyone who owned shares in these companies lost money, a lot of it—which reminds me of another story.

Years ago, an older woman had an appointment to see me for the first time. As she walked into my office, dressed in black, tissue in hand, wiping away her tears, she said, "I doubt you can help me. I was hoping against hope that I was reading this statement incorrectly." As she handed me her brokerage statement, she told me her husband had just passed away and that she had never been involved in any of their financial decisions. When I examined the brokerage account, it had a balance of less than $100. The widow went on to say that her husband had invested their entire life savings in Enron stock. What used to be a half-million-dollar account was now worth just about nothing.

I wish I could describe the look on her face when I confirmed they had lost all their money; she was broke. I can't imagine what that must have felt like. She was elderly, widowed, and penniless.

So, why is a diversified portfolio paramount? Number one, because it's biblical. In Ecclesiastes 11:2 (NIV), Solomon said:

> Invest in seven ventures, yes, in eight; you do not know
> what disaster may come upon the land.

Why diversify? Because you would be crazy not to. There is no perfect investment and no way to avoid risk completely.

The purpose of diversification is to maximize your return by investing in different asset classes that do not react the same when a tragedy occurs. Diversification can be the most critical component of reaching your long-term financial goals while minimizing risk.

Why diversify? Because risk can be hidden and is often unquantifiable. One of the most significant risks we face is that of an unknown future event like 9/11 and how such an event might affect our investments.

> There's a big difference between probability and outcome. Probable things fail to happen, and improbable things happen all the time. That's the most important thing you can know about investment risk.
>
> —HOWARD MARKS

Imagine owning airline stocks on September 10, 2001. Many airlines filed for bankruptcy protection; some went out of business after the horrific events of September 11. Those who survived saw their share prices decline by 70 to 90% in the following months. That's only one reason you should take Solomon's advice and not put all your eggs in one basket.

Proper diversification can help reduce risk and volatility by investing in multiple noncorrelated asset classes (stocks, bonds, commodities, etc.).[32] It can smooth out some of the bumps in the road that you're bound to face.

Stocks may be the top-performing asset class this year, REITs the next year, and fixed index annuities the following year. None of us can know the future with any degree of certainty. Therefore, buying multiple (seven to eight, as Solomon suggests) investments can assure us of having some of our investment dollars in the right place at the right time. With a diversified portfolio that suits your risk tolerance and long-term investment objectives, you may be able to live happily ever after.

If you do not properly diversify, you may end up in my next book as another horror story.

---

32 The price of one asset class has little or no effect on the price of another asset class.

Before we look at a couple of model portfolios used by two of the greatest minds in finance, let's deal with risk and volatility. They are not the same thing.

Unlike just about everything, investment **risk** has no universally accepted definition.

But for the sake of convenience, let's go with Webster: "the possibility … that something bad or unpleasant will happen."

It seems like something unpleasant happens every decade or so in the investment world. The crash of 1987, the events of 9/11, the "Great Recession" of December 2007 to June 2009, and the awful pandemic of 2020 all created deep downturns in the stock market. Here's the problem with risk: we don't know when the next unpleasant event will happen or what it will be. Because our financial system and markets are dynamic, nonlinear, uncertain, and complex, and we lack perfect information, we cannot know the probabilities or likelihood of the next bad thing.

The bottom line is that risk is unknowable and non-quantifiable. Risk is the possibility of permanent loss. So be prepared—be ready—be diversified.

Remember, we never get a second chance to undo a permanent loss!

Volatility, on the other hand, has more to do with an investment's daily, weekly, monthly, or annual price change. The more the price fluctuates, the greater the volatility.

Never confuse risk with volatility. The press and academics often use the terms interchangeably, which is inaccurate.

Allow me to beat a dead horse. Repeat after me: risk and volatility are not the same thing. It is crucial to distinguish between the two. Why? Because investors who learn how to ride out times of volatility without selling avoid a permanent loss. Got it?

David Swensen, Yale University's previous chief investment officer, was responsible for managing and investing Yale's endowment fund and other assets totaling 27 billion dollars. Under the "Swensen Approach," the Yale endowment fund was a top performer among Ivy League schools[33] with a 20-year average annual return of 12.1%.[34] David has also authored two books on investing and portfolio management. Both are worth reading, assuming you don't mind reading books by a very smart guy with ten initials after his name! Swensen suggests stocks from developed and emerging markets from around the world as well as owning real estate and treasuries, including traditional U.S. Treasury bonds and treasury inflation-protected securities (TIPS).

David Swensen Portfolio

This is David Swensen's basic model for creating an investment portfolio likely to produce good returns while still managing risk:

1. Domestic Equity (30%): Refers to stocks in U.S.-based companies listed on U.S. exchanges.
2. Emerging Market Equity (5%): Refers to stocks from emerging markets around the world, such as Brazil, Russia, India, and China.
3. Foreign Developed Equity (15%): Refers to stocks listed on major foreign markets in developed countries, such as the United Kingdom, Germany, France, and Japan.
4. Real Estate Investment Trusts (20%): Refers to stocks of companies that invest directly in real estate through ownership of property.
5. U.S. Treasury Notes and Bonds (15%): These are fixed-interest U.S. government debt securities that mature in more than one

---

33 According to Institutional Investor

34 Source: Yale Investment Office

year. Notes and bonds pay interest semi-annually. The income is taxed only at the federal level.

6. U.S. Treasury Inflation-Protection Securities, or TIPS (15%): These are special types of Treasury notes that offer protection from inflation (as measured by the Consumer Price Index). They pay interest every six months and the principal back to you when the security matures.

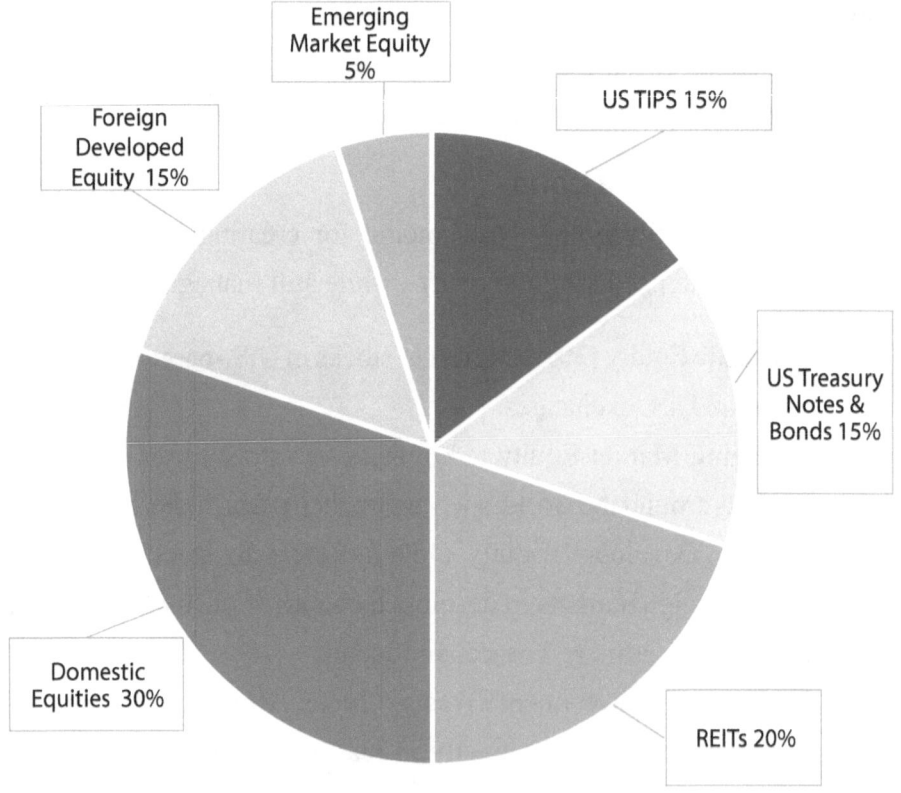

Swensen also stresses the importance of keeping fees low.

So, if you want to invest like a Yalie, this model portfolio is a smart way to go.

Ray Dalio, the second mind worth picking, is the founder of Bridgewater Associates, one of the world's largest and most successful hedge funds. Ray also authored a best-selling book called *Principles*.

Dalio generally requires his clients to have at least 7.5 billion dollars of investable assets to put money into his fund. Since most of us don't have that kind of dough[35] lying around, I thought I would share his portfolio recommendations from a recently published book so you can do it yourself. He takes a different approach than Swensen. His "All Weather" portfolio includes gold and commodities but no real estate.

Incidentally, I didn't feel it was all that important to dedicate an entire chapter to commodities. Why? Because commodities are simply—commodities. Oil, gold, wheat, coffee, sugar, and silver fit into the category.

The returns on commodities are well below that of other investment asset classes. There are, however, good reasons to consider adding them to a portfolio when the time is right—diversification being one. They do not necessarily react to world and economic events the same way stocks or bonds might.

I used gold as an investment alternative only once in my career. I have always felt there are only two good reasons to own gold: Number one, when there is hyperinflation (like we had in the Jimmy Carter years), and number two, when there is political uncertainty. The events of September 11 qualify for the latter, as does the Iranian Hostage Crisis in 1979 (when the price of precious metals skyrocketed).

Our firm added a gold mutual fund to our clients' accounts weeks after the attack on NYC and then sold the fund a couple of years later.

---

35 Another Wall Street technical term

The result? Over a 100% profit! A word of caution is in order, however. I have not bought gold since. There has been no good reason to do so since 9/11. Thank God!

Remember, there is a time to buy and a time to sell. I choose not to deal with stock futures, options, and currency trading, which is more along the lines of speculation and requires specialized training and expertise to lose a significant amount of one's money.

I also refuse to deal with the crypto craze. Charlie Munger called it an "investment in nothing" and "rat poison", saying that investors would have to be "almost insane" to consider buying it. Mr. Munger also said many other nasty things about crypto not fit for me to print. He strongly urged investors to avoid it. If you're wondering why, google "crypto bankruptcies". You could spend the rest of your life reading the 1,250,000 results. Sounds like fun, huh? Oh, and by the way, Fox News recently reported that Tom Brady invested $30 million in FTX and was an "ambassador" for the cryptocurrency exchange. It's all gone now.

I've seen way too many Christians embrace cryptocurrency even though they don't understand it or how it works. They simply see it as a get-rich-quick scheme. Unfortunately, more often than not, investing in crypto turns out to be a get-poor-quick scheme.

Here's a friendly reminder from Solomon:

> A faithful person will be richly blessed, but one **eager to get rich** will not go unpunished.
> — PROVERBS 28:20 NIV

Back to what Dalio's All Weather Fund looks like.

Surprisingly, the largest percentage is allocated to bonds. Since bonds are theoretically less risky and volatile than stocks, Dalio takes a more conservative approach.

According to the available data, Ray's All Weather Portfolio would have had a 9.72%[36] average annualized return over a 30-year period, with only four negative years. The worst year was -3.93% in 2008, when the S&P 500 was down 37%. Very impressive!

This is what Ray Dalio's All Weather Portfolio looks like:

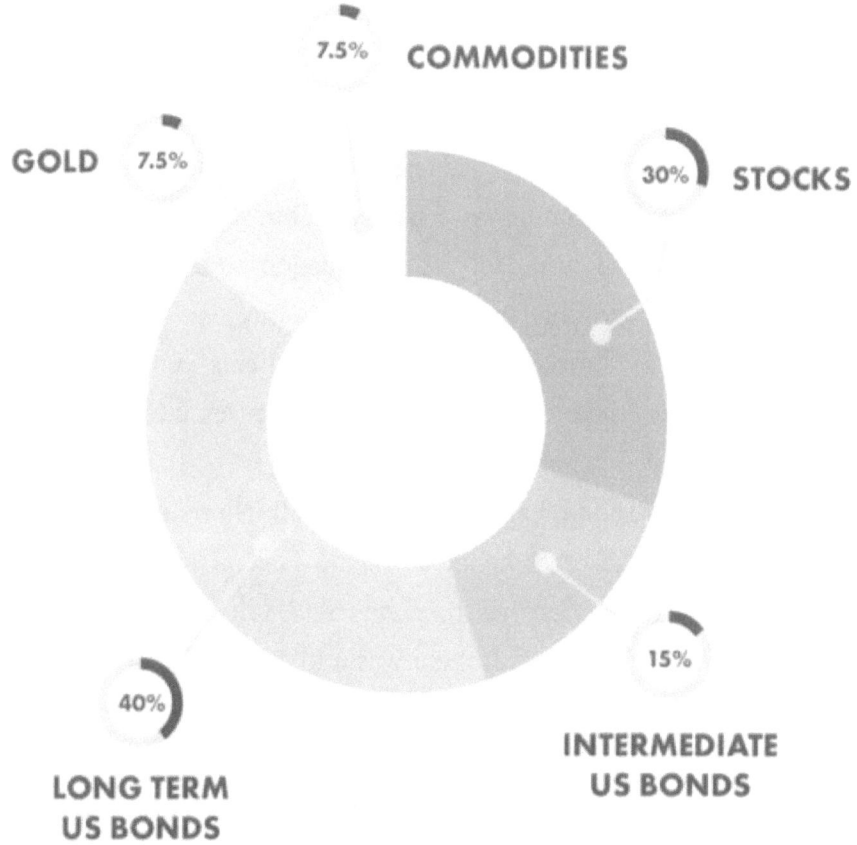

7.5% COMMODITIES

GOLD   7.5%

30% STOCKS

40%

LONG TERM
US BONDS

15%

INTERMEDIATE
US BONDS

If you are more on the unadventurous side and desire to sleep well, Ray Dalio's All Weather Portfolio may be just the right asset allocation for you.

As a money manager, I took a different approach. Remember, there is no magic formula—no single investment or asset model that is perfect for everyone. I was managing portfolios long before Swensen and Dalio became famous and published their books. I'm also old enough to have seen it all:[37] crashes, recessions, terrorist attacks, COVID-19, assassinations, wars, and rumors of wars. Unfortunately, I am no longer young enough to know everything. Once my children grew up, they told me how little I knew!

My point is that I wanted more flexibility when I managed my clients' money. There is no such thing as one portfolio that is ideal for every human on the planet—contrary to what Dave Ramsey preaches. Getting locked into a fixed, rigid model with no freedom to take advantage of changing market conditions makes no sense to me.

Being forced to allocate 40 to 50% of my clients' money in bonds because the model says I must (when the Fed raises interest rates) is economic suicide. A smarter strategy would be to get out of bonds altogether and invest in other assets that do well in a rising interest rate environment. On the other hand, when the Federal Reserve lowered interest rates thirteen times after the events of 9/11, it became abundantly clear (even to Mr. Magoo) that there was a lot of money to be made in bonds. Remember, when interest rates go down, bond values increase, and vice versa. Another great example would be the Great Recession of 2008. As the stock market was getting trashed, the prudent thing to do would have been to reduce your equity positions and move elsewhere.

Diversification is extremely important. But in my mind, so is the ability to make changes when bad things happen and take advantage of opportunities when they present themselves.

---

37 Including dinosaurs roaming the earth!

My templates[38] gave me a lot of flexibility to maneuver as market conditions changed. So, this is the model I used when I managed a growth and income portfolio: I would start by allocating a percentage in small-cap stocks (companies worth less than $1 billion) or small-cap mutual funds, a portion in mid-cap stocks (companies worth $1 to $8 billion) or mid-cap mutual funds, a percentage in large-cap stocks (companies worth over $8 billion) or large-cap mutual funds, an amount in international stocks or international stock funds, and a portion in bonds or bond funds and real estate investment trusts. The exact percentage or allocation was based on the individual client's profile and risk tolerance.

By investing in small, medium, and large capitalized stocks and/or MFs, I could avoid overlap and duplication in my clients' portfolios. You obviously won't find a small-cap stock in a large-cap mutual fund, thus achieving pure diversification. (More on that subject in the Dave Ramsey chapter.)

Because I was a registered investment advisor, or RIA (see the next chapter), I had the discretion to make changes in my clients' portfolios as necessary. Here's why that's important: mutual funds are categorized as growth, value, or blend by Morningstar. If the economy was doing well, I would use growth funds. If the economy started to cool, value funds might be the more appropriate place to be invested. If the bond market was getting destroyed because of multiple rate hikes, I could move out of bonds and go elsewhere. I wasn't locked into keeping money in a declining asset class. I could also lower or raise the percentages in any given asset based on what was happening in the world.

For example, the Dow Jones Industrial Average returned 56% during Trump's first term. When the stock market is moving up because of

---

38 I used growth, aggressive growth, growth and income, income, and conservative portfolio models, depending on my client's risk profile.

anticipated economic growth, why shouldn't I (as a money manager) try to take advantage of having a larger percentage of my clients' money in growth stocks?

So, how should your portfolio be allocated? It depends. It all boils down to what you are comfortable with. Do you want to sleep well or eat well? Fidelity and Vanguard offer numerous portfolio models on their websites. Both show various risk/reward illustrations that may be very helpful to you in deciding how much risk you might be willing to take.

Don't Lose Your Balance

Almost every investment professional agrees you should rebalance your portfolio regularly, either quarterly or annually. Rebalancing simply means the periodic buying and selling of your assets to maintain your original allocation. Why should you rebalance? Say your stock portion performed extremely well over the past couple of years. Stocks have now become a higher percentage of your original allocation. In other words, if your initial allocation was 50% stocks and 50% bonds, you may now be allocated 70% stocks and 30% bonds. This may result in more risk than you would be comfortable with. When you rebalance, you sell the overweighted portion and relocate it to the underweighted asset, bringing it back to a 50/50 split. Make sense?

This strategy forces you to adhere to a timeless investment principle: buy low, sell high. Next time you find yourself a little off-balance, make sure you fix it before you regret it.

Now that you know what diversification is and why it's important, let's be crystal clear on what diversification is not. It's not owning three equity mutual funds, five CDs at different banks, or four annuities with various insurance companies.

If you own more than one mutual fund that owns many of the same stocks in each of their portfolios, you are not diversified! If you own multiple rental properties that make up most of your net worth, you are not diversified. What will happen to you the next time we encounter another real estate collapse like we did in 2006 through 2012? Don't make the same mistake the widow's husband I mentioned earlier made by investing everything in one stock. Don't put all or most of your investable assets in a solitary asset class. You are asking for trouble if you don't heed the wisdom of the ancients: *invest in seven ventures, yes in eight; you do not know what disaster may come.* **Never, ever become desensitized to risk.**

Ever wonder who the most famous female financier was in the Bible? Moses's mother! Why? She went to the bank and floated a prophet! Along the same lines, Zechariah and Elizabeth made a prophet when John the Baptist was born.

Here's another multiplication example from the Bible:

> When Isaac planted his crops that year, he harvested a hundred times more than he planted, for The Lord blessed him.
>
> — GENESIS 26:12 (NLT)

How awesome is that?

8.
GETTING SOUND INVESTMENT ADVICE

I am often asked for investment tips by family and friends. My response is almost always the same.[39] Prescribing without proper diagnosis is malpractice. No two people are identical, and similarly, no two investors are the same.

What are your financial goals? What is your time horizon? What is your risk tolerance?

These are but a few of the essential factors that need to be crystallized before sound investment advice can be given. If someone gives you a tip without asking these questions first, run! Be very careful to whom you listen! You cannot rely on fools, friends, or family for sound investment advice.

So, where do you go for reliable financial advice? **An insurance agent?** What do insurance agents sell? Insurance products. Are insurance products the right investment for everybody? Of course not. Most of

---

these guys aren't licensed to recommend or sell stocks, bonds, or mutual funds. What happens if stocks are the best solution for your investment needs? They still try to sell you insurance products because that's all they have to sell, even if it's not the right product for you. That's not good; it's a clear conflict of interest.

Especially beware of the "captive agent." That's an insurance agent who works for only one company, which means they can only offer insurance products from a single company, regardless of whether they are good, bad, or just plain ugly. Having an insurance agent come to my home to do a sales presentation is not my idea of a fun-filled evening. I am reminded of a scene from my favorite Woody Allen movie, *Take the Money and Run*, where he is sentenced to ten years locked in solitary confinement with an insurance salesman. Pretty harsh, don't you think? A clear violation of the 8th Amendment, dealing with cruel and unusual punishment.

Speaking of prison, ever wonder why the French celebrate Bastille Day, which commemorates the storming of the Bastille on July 14, 1789? They are the only country I know of that celebrates breaking *into* prison. Very strange.

If you need insurance, buy it from a good, reputable agent[40] and company. If you need investment products, go elsewhere.

What about banks? Banks employ licensed salespeople who sell CDs and annuities; some offer mutual funds. Who are these people sitting behind the desk offering investment products? Here's my take: the average Wall Street salary is over $400,000 a year. I think you'll agree the average pay for a bank employee is somewhat less than 400k. So, why are these investment people working at a bank (making much

---

40 My insurance agent, Steve Lane, has three daughters: Diane, Lois, and Penny.

less money) instead of a major Wall Street firm? Because most are below-average investment advisers. I'm not disparaging them. They are probably very good people. They are just not your best option for investment advice.

Some of these folks were bank tellers who were encouraged to get a mutual fund license (Series 6) despite the fact they had no prior investment experience. Getting a Series 6 license is pretty easy, but getting a license doesn't make someone a pro. I have a driver's license, but I am not a professional driver, nor am I qualified to enter the Indy 500. Be careful! If the only license I had was to sell mutual funds, what would I try to sell you? That's a conflict of interest, wouldn't you say? A very large misconception regarding buying mutual funds and variable annuities from banks is that by doing so, you get FDIC insurance. That is simply not true. Investment products are not insured by the federal government or anyone else, and you can lose money. Unfortunately, banks often forget to disclose this minor detail.

Another pitfall of buying mutual funds from a bank is that most banks have limited selling agreements with mutual fund companies. In other words, a bank may offer you only a minimal selection of mutual funds. I would rather make my investment choices from the entire fund universe and not be limited to just a couple of options. I urge caution before buying investment products from a bank. They work on commission, and you pay a fee (hidden or otherwise), regardless of whether you make money. These sometimes ethically challenged salespeople are neither financially responsible nor accountable for the advice they give you. A word of advice from your author: no matter who you end up working with in the investment field, make sure they have at least ten years of experience. It takes that long to become a seasoned professional. Don't let a novice cut their teeth on your life savings.

Please forgive me for adopting a tone of righteous indignation, but for the uninitiated, investing with a rookie can be an easy way for the gullible and imprudent to lose their hard-earned money.

How does working with a stockbroker sound? To say their interests are the same as yours would be a lie. A broker who receives a commission for every trade they make is acting in direct conflict with your best interest. Here's how the game is played. A stockbroker sells you 100 shares of IBM because the firm's analyst thinks it's a good buy. A few months later, the broker's mortgage payment is past due, and he needs to make a sale/commission sooner rather than later. Your broker calls you and says: "You know, that IBM stock I sold you has done really well. Why don't we sell it, take the profit, and buy Southwest Airlines?[41] I think it's ready to take off" (pun intended). You take his advice because, after all, he's the expert. What just happened? You paid your broker three commissions: one to buy IBM, one to sell IBM, and another to buy Southwest Airlines, which you will eventually end up selling someday when his kids go off to college, making it a total of four paychecks for your Wall Street wizard. Or, on the other hand, if IBM goes down instead of up, your broker calls and says something like this: "You know that IBM stock you bought a while ago? Sorry, it didn't work out for you. The analyst who recommended the stock is no longer with our firm. Our new analyst is awesome, and she recommends Southwest Airlines. Why don't we sell IBM and cut your losses and buy Southwest before it hits new highs?" Either way, whether you made money or not, the broker ends up making moolah[42] four times. Never

---

41 I was on a flight from Raleigh-Durham airport to Newark when the co-pilot told us over the PA system that his name was Parish, the pilot's name was Graves, and we were about to leave the terminal.

42 Wall Street technical term

forget that they don't get paid to make you money; they get paid to sell investment products. The more they sell, the more money they make. Never succumb to a self-serving sales pitch. Make investment decisions when you are ready, not under pressure. To repeat—brokers are not on your side.

By the way, the word *broker* comes from the Saxon word *broc,* which means misfortune. The Oxford Dictionary tells us that between the years 1377 and 1690, the word *broker* meant, among other things: procurer, pimp, bawd, and panderer.

Here's something else to ponder: It takes six months for a beautician to become licensed and two years for a plumber to become certified to unclog your toilet. It only takes four to five months to become a stockbroker. That's frightening, wouldn't you say? Here's my last critique of Wall Street and stockbrokers. In 2012, the large investment firms laid off roughly 75,000 human beings. In the same year, cash bonuses paid to the big shots running these firms was $19.7 billion. Gordon Gekko may think greed is good, but I doubt the 75,000 families who lost their livelihood would agree.

OK, humor me with just a few more jabs. Richard Whitney, President of the New York Stock Exchange in the 1930s, once said, "One of the prime necessities of a great market is that brokers must be honest and financially responsible." As it turns out, he was neither. Mr. Whitney, the Bernie Madoff of his time, was later convicted of embezzlement and sentenced to five to ten years in Sing Sing prison.[43] He ended up a jailbird and died broke.

---

43 The phrase 'up the river' originally came from going to prison at Sing Sing, which is up the Hudson River from NYC.

A few quotes on these wheeler-dealers are in order:

> Wall Street is the only place where people ride in a Rolls-Royce to get advice from people who take the subway.
> — WARREN BUFFETT

> The brokerage industry services investors like Bonnie and Clyde service banks.
> — WILLIAM BERNSTEIN

> I'd compare stock pickers to astrologers, but I don't want to bad-mouth astrologers.
> — EUGENE FAMA, AMERICAN ECONOMIST

Warning! Anyone can call themselves a **financial planner**. It's a title, not a professional designation. A banker, insurance agent, or stockbroker can call themselves a financial planner or financial advisor. Calling somebody something doesn't necessarily make it so. According to a study done by the Financial Planning Association, 46% of financial planners have no retirement plan. That should tell you something.

My first and only experience with a financial planner was back in 1985. I had an appointment with a guy who worked with IDS, which was bought by American Express and later spun off to become Ameriprise Financial. I wanted to open an IRA for my wife and me in a mutual fund. The so-called financial planner convinced me to invest our IRA money into a limited partnership instead of mutual funds. I figured he knew more than I did because he was a financial planner! As it turned out, it only took my expert planner a couple of years to lose the entire investment.

I just took a couple of minutes to calculate how much our $4,000 IRA money would have grown if it had been invested in the S&P 500 Index over the past 3.8 decades. Sad to say, it would have been worth just shy of $100,000 today. I should have known better than to take financial advice from someone still working for a living.

Nothing is more difficult than succeeding in the investment arena, yet it is attempted by so many poorly trained individuals. As far as I am concerned, it is nearly impossible for ordinary investors to outperform the market because there is so much incompetence in the financial industry.

So, where do we turn for expert investment guidance? Let's explore what a Registered Investment Advisor (RIA) is and what they do.

RIAs are fiduciaries[44] and are held to a higher standard than other investment professionals by the U.S. Securities and Exchange Commission (SEC). They are legally and ethically required to put the client's needs above their own at all times. A fiduciary is a person to whom property or power is entrusted for the benefit of another. An RIA is paid solely for advice, accepting no commissions for investment products.

There are no conflicts of interest; the client and the RIA sit on the same side of the table with their interests aligned. In contrast, commission-driven salespeople (bankers, brokers, and insurance agents) are not fiduciaries; they are not held to the same legal standards as RIAs. Most RIAs are independent; they are not tied to any specific family of mutual funds, exchange-traded funds, real estate investment trusts, or any other investment products. They can do their own research and recommend what they consider to be the very best opportunities for their clients.

---

44 A fiduciary is a formal word meaning "relating to or involving trust (such as trust between a customer and a professional)" (Merriam-Webster).

Here are a number of important benefits for those working with a registered investment advisor:

1. Your money is held by an independent custodian, not the RIA advisor's firm. Remember Bernie Madoff's famous last words before he made off with his clients' money? "In today's environment, it's virtually impossible to violate rules."

2. Expertise. Most RIAs specialize and focus on investment strategies.

3. Customized guidance—tailored to what's best for you and your family.

4. A transparent and simple fee structure. You are charged a fee based on a percentage of assets managed by your RIA.

5. RIAs are focused on building deep, ongoing relationships with their clients, involving regular interactions.

6. Tax advantages. The fee you pay an RIA may be tax-deductible. So, a 1.5% advisory fee could be closer to 1% when you consider the deduction. Compare that with a 2%, or higher, fee you pay to a mutual fund manager (more on that later) that is not tax-deductible.

7. Accountability. You can fire your RIA at any time. If they don't live up to your expectations or deliver as promised, you can hand them a pink slip and move on.

8. Client accounts are covered by the Securities Investor Protection Corporation (SIPC)[45] with a limit of $500,000, which includes a $250,000 limit on cash for theft, fraud, or misuse of your money.

---

45 The SIPC does not cover market loss or investment products that are not registered with the Securities and Exchange Commission.

As you can tell, I am a fan of Registered Investment Advisors. They must, by law, put their clients' interests above their own (unlike just about everyone else in the financial industry). May I remind you that I am retired. I have no products to sell, ax to grind, or hidden agenda. I am giving you my honest opinion. You take it from there. I also think most investors need professional help. I've seen too many people self-destruct by going it alone. Even Han Solo had a copilot!

> Successful investing is elusive. If it weren't, everybody would be shopping on Rodeo Drive.
> — FROM *THE WEALTHY BARBER*

I assure you that the stock market will eventually teach you a lesson or two. The market can make fools out of most investors on a fairly regular basis. Unfortunately, these lessons can be very costly. At the end of the day, for most folks, there is no way spending a few hours a week looking at various investment products will equip you to compete with the incredibly talented, highly qualified, extremely well-educated individuals who spend their entire professional careers in finance. It's not a fair fight.

Most individual investors possess neither the time nor resources to succeed in managing their portfolios. The markets are dominated by sophisticated institutional investors, making it extremely difficult to win the investment game.

My main point here is that the amateur investor has numerous disadvantages in relation to the professional. Recognizing this reality, even if you don't like it (especially if you don't like it), will help you a great deal in the long run. Here's why: according to a recent study done by Aon Hewitt, advice seekers retire with 79% more money than the typical investor. I think you'll agree that's a big deal. But wait, there's more.[46] According to the Vanguard Group, an investment advisory firm, a good advisor can bring considerable monetary value to your portfolio—3.75% per year in added value by lowering your fees, increasing performance, and incorporating behavioral coaching. RIAs help guide you through market declines and extreme volatility. They help you stay the course and focus on your long-term goals instead of short-term events that may distract you.

Think of it this way. My wife and I love to travel. We have been just about everywhere on Earth, including the North Pole. How wise would I be if I took off for 90° north without a guide? I doubt I would be around to write this book. Whenever we travel to a foreign country, we take a guided tour or hire our own tour guide ahead of time. It makes our vacation easier to navigate and far less stressful. I would submit to you that hiring an investment professional would give you the same gratification and peace of mind.

> A mountain climber who disclaims the aid of a guide can expect no other epitaph than that he deserves. The penalty of extreme folly!
> — ARTHUR CRUMP

I had a long and successful career in the investment business, mainly as a Registered Investment Advisor. I saw a lot of stuff happen over my professional lifetime: a pandemic, wars, recessions, and a stock market crash. But nothing had a deeper impact on my professional life than the events of September 11, 2001. To this day, I still vividly remember watching the Twin Towers in New York City come down as my staff huddled in my office to catch a glimpse of the television. To say the events of 9/11 were traumatic would be a gross understatement. I lost

---

46 I feel a free Ginsu Knife offer coming soon.

friends, neighbors, and colleagues that day. My staff looked at me with uncertain eyes and asked, "What now?"

As an RIA, I had a legal responsibility to do what I thought was right for my 1,700 clients. I managed a lot of money for a lot of people back in the day. Many had become close friends. I also had a moral obligation to take action so these folks wouldn't get hurt financially. There was no doubt in my mind that the stock market would get clobbered whenever it reopened. I prayed for wisdom and guidance. After a couple of days, it became clear to me what action I should take: sell everything. We sold every stock and stock mutual fund and went to cash the moment the stock market resumed trading on September 17, 2001. As an RIA, I was able to have our traders push a single button and sell all our clients' equity positions before the market saw its biggest losses (for a single week) in history, nearly 15%. After things settled down, we were able to buy back some of the very same investments we owned months earlier at a substantial discount, making our clients a lot of money. On the other hand, most brokers gave their clients the following advice: "Hang in there; the market will come back!" When? Three, five, ten years? Imagine a 70-year-old retiree waiting ten years to break even!

I tell you this story because a trusted adviser or counselor (a consigliere) can be worth their weight in gold. Finding the best person or firm to invest your money is one of the most important financial decisions you'll ever make. Seek honest, capable, expert guidance—someone you like and trust. Your financial future depends on it! Expecting to make a large sum of money on your own with only a small amount of investment knowledge is like expecting to shoot a great round of golf the first time you visit the course.

This seems like an excellent place to end. In the next chapter, we will discuss investors behaving badly.

Any idea who the greatest investor in the Bible was? Noah—while his stock was rising, everyone else was in liquidation! Before we move on, I want to share another story from the Bible that illustrates how our God is in the multiplication business:

> [32]Jesus called his disciples to him and said: "I have compassion for these people; they have already been with me three days and have nothing to eat. I do not want to send them away hungry, or they may collapse on the way." [33]His disciples answered, "Where could we get enough bread in this remote place to feed such a crowd?" [34]"How many loaves do you have?" Jesus asked. "Seven," they replied, "and a few small fish." [35]He told the crowd to sit down on the ground. [36]Then he took the seven loaves and the fish, and when he had given thanks, he broke them and gave them to the disciples, and they in turn to the people. [37]They all ate and were satisfied. Afterward, the disciples picked up seven basketfuls of broken pieces that were left over. [38]The number of those who ate was four thousand men, besides women and children.

> — Matthew 15:32–38 (NIV)

The point is Jesus can use what little we have and multiply it, too.

9.
BEHAVE YOURSELF

This chapter is rated "MA" for mature audiences only. *The truth? You can't handle the truth!*[47]

> The investor's chief problem—and even his worst enemy—is likely to be himself.
>
> —BENJAMIN GRAHAM,
> AUTHOR OF *THE INTELLIGENT INVESTOR*

If you are not doing well as an investor, maybe *you* are the culprit. My primary reason for writing this chapter is to help you minimize future regret.

More and more studies are confirming the obvious: most individual investors act irrationally. The problem is they don't know they are irrational. When the average investor gets clobbered in the stock market, they tend to blame it on somebody or something else.

---

47 A quote from the movie, A Few Good Men

My barber said it was a sure thing. I didn't know the Fed was going to raise interest rates. How was I supposed to know Toys "R" Us would file for bankruptcy?

The finger of blame almost always points elsewhere. Investors must take responsibility for their investment decisions and not seek a scapegoat. In all likelihood, the problem is not the stock market, it's our behavior. Throughout my career, I have seen so many people make the dumbest stock selections, such as buying shares in a "chicken ranch" (brothel) in Nevada, penny stocks in an Angola gold mine, and GM a week before it filed for bankruptcy because it was "too big to fail." Nonsense—this last guy was watching too much CNBC. I warned this young chap that no company was too big to fail, and it made perfect sense for GM to file for Chapter 11 due to costly pension and other long-term retiree obligations.

Sure enough, despite my warning, he bought several hundred shares of GM, and sure enough, a week later, they went bust. My inexperienced, dumb advice seeker lost his shirt. Meanwhile, the alternative investment I recommended to him worked out quite nicely, thank you. More often than not, we are our own worst enemy.

> I can calculate the motion of heavenly bodies, but not the madness of people.
> — SIR ISAAC NEWTON

> By definition, risk-takers often fail. So do morons. In practice, it's difficult to sort them out.
> — SCOTT ADAMS

Fear and greed are two of the most dangerous traits to have as an investor. I have two examples of how treacherous these flaws can be.

The first is a client who was upset with me because she only made 50% in her mutual funds when her friend made 200% in a tech fund. After switching to her friend's technology fund, my ex-client lost most of her money the following year in the dot-com bomb. I haven't heard from her since. The second is the widow whose husband invested all their money in the Enron stock I cited earlier. Greed is not good. Jesus warns us to: "Watch Out! Be on your guard against all kinds of greed."[48] Greed can help you lose your money in a hurry. Fear, on the other hand, can keep you from making money when opportunities arise.

I am reminded of a conversation I had with a couple of pastor friends of mine back in 2009. They wanted to know what I thought the market would do—as if I had access to some sort of psychic hotline. Remember, the S&P 500 was down 37% in 2008. Also, remember that I invested most of the cash I was sitting on from the sale of my practice in blue chip stocks in the spring of 2009. I told them I thought the market had probably hit bottom, and it might be a good time to buy. Their response was perplexing. "Are you nuts?" they asked. They then began to rattle off a list of everything that was wrong with our economy and the stock market.

Fear kept them out of the market. They ended up wasting a golden opportunity (buying low)[49] to make a lot of money.

---

48 Luke 12:15 (NIV)

49 I often have unoriginal thoughts.

Whoever watches the wind will not plant; whoever looks at the clouds will not reap...

Sow your seed in the morning, and in the evening, let your hands not be idle, for you do not know which will succeed, whether this or that, or whether both will do equally well.

ECCLESIASTES 11:4,6

Ecclesiastes is warning us not to wait for ideal or perfect conditions before we act. We live in an imperfect and uncertain world. In fact, the more uncertainty there is in the investment world, the more likely there are tremendous buying opportunities.

Since my conversation with these gentlemen, the S&P 500 is up over 200%—a truly rewarding experience for this author and his family. Not so much for my two friends. The important thing to remember is that the stock market has recovered and moved on to new highs after each and every crash, correction, recession, and crisis.

Never forget the importance of that statement. These temporary downturns can be terrific buying opportunities.

Look at market fluctuations as your friend rather than your enemy. Profit from folly rather than participate in it.

— WARREN BUFFETT

Remember, your success (or lack thereof) is directly correlated to the price you pay. The lower the price you pay for a quality asset, the higher the upside potential and the lower the downside risk. Got it? It never ceases to amaze me why most Americans will not buy stocks and bonds when they go on sale.

Fear can be paralyzing and detrimental to your investment success. One of my family members e-mailed me early in the morning after Mr. Trump was elected president in 2015. Her question: "Should I get out of the market and go to cash?" My response: "Why?" She was afraid of what might happen to her 401(k). I sent her a lengthy response on how the stock market might react negatively to the new president in the short term, but in the long term, it should move higher because of anticipated increased corporate earnings, lower taxes, and economic growth. Politics don't impact the markets in the long run—earnings and profits do.

As it turned out, we did a family reunion trip to Disney World two years later. I asked her what she ended up doing with her 401(k). I was delighted to hear she ended up doing nothing. The good news for her is the Dow Jones Industrial Average has doubled since Inauguration Day 2016! All's well that ends well.

I recall a phone conversation with my trade desk back in 2009. That's when I started buying stocks because the Dow Jones Industrial Average went below 7,000 for the first time in many years. A very tempting entry point. My first question to them was, "Is anyone buying?" They laughed. "Only sellers," they said. In my mind, that was a clear indicator (I'm a contrarian) that it was indeed a good time to get back into the market. I've also tried to take Jesus at His word when He said: "Engage in business until I come."[50] The Bible also tells us at least 80 times to *fear not*. It is great advice for investing and living life to its fullest.

The problem is that most people do not recognize or admit to being irrational. Waiting for the stock market to recover before investing makes absolutely no sense. Why pay full price when you can buy at a discount? Sad to say, just about everyone I know does not act rationally

---

50 Luke 19:13 (ESV)

when it comes to investing. Unfortunately, the rational man—like Big Foot—is often sighted but rarely photographed.

Consider the following:

A recent DALBAR[51] study shows the return of the S&P 500 Index over a 30-year period was 11.11% per annum. Compare that to the average individual investor who only had a 3.69% return per year over the same period. That's a whopping 7.42% difference annually! If you invested $100K at 11.11% for 30 years, you would have $2,358,275.00. The same amount invested at 3.69% over the same period only grew to $296,556.00. That's a disparity of $2,061,719.00—not exactly small change.

So, why does the average investor underperform the market by such a large gap? Because many investors chase performance. They look at a list of top-performing mutual funds and buy what's hot. Thus, once again, they buy high and will eventually sell low once the top performer tanks because of short-term underperformance, which is inevitable. According to Davis Advisors, 95% of the top-performing mutual fund managers fell into the bottom half of their peer groups for at least one three-year period.[52] I hope you get the significance of that statistic. Folks buy a hot fund and dump it when it has a bad year or quarter. Buying high and selling low is a truly lousy investment strategy.

Do it often enough, and you will need to join "Losers Anonymous." Emotions are another problem—a big one. Great investors possess emotional stability. They make their buying and selling decisions on practical, calculated information, not feelings. Reason and logic must always overcome emotion. Just pretend you're British; stay calm and carry on.

---

51 DALBAR Inc. is the nation's leading financial services market research firm.
52 From 2004 through 2013

If you want to be a great investor, you must come to grips with reality. Investing is not gambling; it's not a thrill-seeking trip to the casino. It's serious hard work, not a way of having fun. You will be rewarded or punished depending on how much time, effort, and energy you put into your investment-making decisions. The reality is you will win some, you will lose some, and some will get rained out. Sometimes an investment choice will not go the way you want it to. One dreary conclusion we need to draw is that unknowable situations are inevitable. The difference between an average investor and a great investor is that great ones learn and grow from their mistakes, while average investors are set back by them. Experience can be a good teacher; however, the fees can be quite high if you are not careful!

If you want to be a great investor, you must also tune out the "noise." When the sky is predicted to fall, you can't save it. Relax. This, too, shall pass. According to psychologist Paul Andreassen: "Paying close attention to financial news can lead investors to trade too much and earn lower returns than those who tune out the news."

Or, as Norman Augustine, U.S. aerospace businessman and author, so wisely said, "If stock market experts were so expert, they would be buying stocks, not selling advice." They are human and not infallible. Turn the financial channel off. Listening to an "expert" who made a couple of lucky calls is a great way to get unlucky. They are often wrong, sometimes remarkably so. They rarely have skin in the game and, therefore, don't have to live with the consequences of making bad investment recommendations—you do. They shouldn't tell you what to buy; they should show you what they own in their portfolio and their long-term performance. Follow the numbers, not the noise. Or, to put it more bluntly: avoid taking advice from someone who gives advice for a living. On the other hand, feel free to take as much advice as you want from professional investors, such as Buffett, Munger, and Dalio. If you want to be a great investor, you should stick with a long-term investment strategy and not make short-term investment decisions driven by fear and greed. Never let your emotions and mental biases get in the way of rationality. If you're into instant gratification, investing may not be for you. As the Book of James says: "For he that wavers is like a wave of the sea driven with the wind and tossed. A double-minded man is unstable in all his ways."[53]

> In actual practice, an investor has to guard against many things, and most of all against himself.
> — JESSE LIVERMORE

You must stay the course and pursue your long-term investment goals despite whatever obstacles or criticism you face.

Too good to be true? A few years back, the Securities and Exchange Commission launched a fake website pitching a biohazard detection device and solicited investments in the company. The site claimed that in three months, your investment would be worth more than 100 times your initial investment. Believe it or not, the website received more than 150,000 hits in just three days! As the saying goes: "There's a sucker born every minute." I repeat: one of the biggest obstacles we face as investors is ourselves.

Fear, greed, emotions, and constant wavering can wreak havoc on our hard-earned investment dollars. So, if you want to be a great investor, stop misbehaving. It is one of the greatest dangers investors face. Do some serious soul-searching. Take a good look in a mirror—if you see the problem staring at you, do what the prodigal son did and come to your senses. No one ever made a dime in the stock market by panicking.

---

53 James 1:6 and 8 (KJV 2000)

Nothing defines human beings better than their willingness to do irrational things in the pursuit of phenomenally unlikely payoffs.

— Scott Adams

Speaking of misbehaving, here's one of my favorite one-liners from Groucho Marx: "I made a killing on Wall Street a few years ago. I shot my broker." According to Groucho, he lost $800,000 in the 1929 crash (an enormous sum back then), all of it invested in stocks. There's a lesson or two in that story.

As you know by now, I love closing each chapter with a story from the Bible illustrating how God is in the multiplication business.

This story of The Widow's Oil comes from 2 Kings Chapter 4 verses 1 through 7 (ESV):

> [1]Now the wife of one of the sons of the prophets cried to Elisha, "Your servant my husband is dead, and you know that your servant feared the Lord, but the creditor has come to take my two children to be his slaves." [2]And Elisha said to her, "What shall I do for you? Tell me; what have you in the house?" And she said, "Your servant has nothing in the house except a jar of oil." [3]Then he said, "Go outside, borrow vessels from all your neighbors, empty vessels and not too few. 4 Then go in and shut the door behind yourself and your sons and pour into all these vessels. And when one is full, set it aside." [5]So she went from him and shut the door behind herself and her sons. And as she poured, they brought the vessels to her. [6]When the vessels were full, she said to her son, "Bring me another vessel." And he said to her, "There is

not another." Then the oil stopped flowing. [7]She came and told the man of God, and he said, "Go, sell the oil and pay your debts, and you and your sons can live on the rest."

The point is God used what little she had and multiplied it. She ended up becoming the world's first oil tycoon. He can do the same for you. Be Blessed!

10.
RAMSEY VS. REALITY

I've been teaching an investment course at my church for many years. A comment I often get from my students is: "Dave Ramsey only takes us so far. He has helped us get out of debt and get our financial house in order, but we don't know where to go from there." They want to go beyond Ramsey's advice of "buying a good mutual fund," whatever that means.

I have occasionally listened to Dave's radio show, read most of his books, and even taught his Financial Peace University course. I would have to agree with my students: Dave Ramsey is a great personal money management expert. He is not, however, a qualified investment professional in any way, shape, or form. To be absolutely clear, Dave Ramsey is not licensed or trained to give investment advice.

I said the very same thing about Larry Burkett[54] in my first book, *Whatever Happened to the Promised Land?* 25 years ago—great financial advice, lousy investment advice. In fact, you would not have made any money after taxes and inflation if you had taken Burkett's

---

54 Christian author, radio host, and financial counselor

investment advice over the past 30 years. Bear in mind that this chapter is not a personal attack on Ramsey; he has helped millions of Americans straighten out their finances, for which he should be commended. But he should stick to what he knows and stop giving investment advice. It's potentially dangerous! Dave's investment philosophy, which he shares on his website, is seriously flawed and represents nothing more than his opinion, which is misguided. Take my Jim Cramer example from Chapter 1. He told one of his viewers not to sell his shares in Bear Stearns. Three days later, the stock fell from $159 a share to $2. Cramer expressed his opinion, which turned out to be disastrous for the caller. The problem is the viewer had to pay the consequence, not Jim Cramer. I don't know about you, but I am much more interested in facts than opinions when it comes to investing.

The following is an opinion expressed on Dave's website, DaveRamsey.com: "I always encourage people to choose a good growth stock mutual fund." I am fascinated by this statement. How does one define a good growth stock mutual fund? Is it the top performer for the past year, three years, five years, ten years, or 20 years? If you do a search, you won't find the same fund ranked as a top performer in all these time periods. In other words, you won't necessarily find the top-rated mutual funds for three years ranked highly in a list of top funds for ten or 20 years. So, what time frame do you use? Ramsey doesn't say. Guessing is not a sound investment strategy.

Remember my Russian mutual fund story from Chapter 4? Last quarter's winner can easily end up the next quarter's loser. Or the research I cited from Davis Advisors: "95% of the top-performing managers from 2004 to 2013 fell into the bottom half of their peer groups for at least one three-year period." Get the point? Most top-performing mutual funds end up underperforming sooner or later. Do you recall my Bill Miller story? His fund outperformed the market for an unheard of 15 straight years, only to suffer catastrophic losses because of bad investment decisions. Is that the kind of "good growth stock mutual fund" you want to own? Me neither. Even Morningstar's top-rated equity funds have lagged the market by a wide margin at some point in time. In plain English, the chance that a #1 fund over the past ten years will repeat as #1 in the next ten years is essentially zero. I'm still scratching my head about what, exactly, Ramsey means by "good." Perhaps I should contact a financial astrologer.

> One essential truth about investing is that generally speaking, good results will bring more money to "hot" money managers and strategies, and if allowed to grow unchecked, more money will bring bad performance.
> — HOWARD MARKS

How about a reality check? Index funds beat roughly 90% of all actively managed stock mutual funds. They have substantially lower fees and lower turnover, thus generating less taxes, and they have no front-end sales charges, unlike what Dave recommends—mutual funds that will cost you 4 to 5%. Why pay an upfront commission when you can buy no-load funds and save yourself some serious money? Help me out here: how is paying a 5% upfront sales charge in your best interest? Maybe it has something to do with the radio star aligning himself with brokers who earn commissions selling mutual funds with front-end sales charges? Brokers must pay Dave $549 per month to become an "endorsed local provider." That is an outrageous conflict of interest, wouldn't you say? Whatever happened to full disclosure?

Oh, by the way, you can purchase many loaded funds commission-free on Fidelity's and Schwab's online brokerage sites. Including the ones Dave touts as "good." Don't waste your hard-earned money on useless and irrelevant advice.

"I recommend growth, growth and income, aggressive growth, and international funds."—from DaveRamsey.com. Does putting 100% of your investable assets into stock mutual funds make any sense to you? That is Dave's blanket recommendation to everyone who visits his website. That's absolutely reprehensible.

Whether you are an aggressive or conservative investor, age 30 or 70, retired or 40 years away from retirement, everyone gets the same investment advice.

That's not exactly stellar counsel. How anyone can recommend putting 100% of your money into stocks[55] (regardless of your goals, risk tolerance, and time horizon) is beyond my comprehension. In fact, it's malpractice, which is prescribing without proper diagnosis. It shows he has very little mastery of the investment world. His advice is idealistically distorted, lacking intellectual integrity and any kind of critical thinking. It's just plain caustic investment advice.

Consider the following:

In the 1987 crash, the market was down 33.5%.
In the aftermath of 9/11, the market was down 36.8%.
In the aftermath of the 2007–2009 Great Recession, the market was down 57.6%.
In the COVID-19 stock market downturn of 2020, the DOW was down 37%.

If you had followed Ramsey's advice, you would have gotten creamed in those bear markets. Who do you know that would be OK with losing half their money? Anyone in their right mind should avoid putting all

---

55 A stock mutual fund is nothing more than a portfolio of individual stocks.

their money in the stock market. Let's do some quick math. If you went with Ramsey's recommendation and lost 50% of your portfolio from 2007 through 2009, the stock market would have to go up 100% for you to break even.

$100,000 investment

- 50% loss

= $50,000 portfolio value

$50,000 portfolio value

+ 100% gain ($50,000)

= $100,000

How long might it take for the market to go up 100% for you to break even?

Three years, five years, ten years? Only God knows. Ramsey states in *Total Money Makeover*: "Your financial process and principles must work in good times and in bad times—otherwise, they don't work." If what Mr. Ramsey states is true, his own investment advice is severely lacking. I wouldn't call losing half my money a successful investment strategy, would you?

Dave's advice on splitting your investment dollars among four stock funds is not biblical! Remember what Solomon said: *Divide your portion to seven, even to eight, for you do not know what misfortune may occur on the earth.* I will take the ancient wisdom of Solomon over Ramsey any day.

Dave's advice defies common sense and my grandmother's wisdom of not putting all your eggs in one basket. If you take Ramsey's advice, that's exactly what you're doing—putting 100% of your hard-earned money into the stock market. As a side note, I was a chief compliance officer early in my career. In my professional opinion, Dave's investment tips are not suitable for most of the people on Planet Earth.

Let's dig deeper into his recommendations. Putting your money in four mutual funds (as Dave suggests) does not give you any degree of real diversification. I went to the mutual fund company's website that most people think Ramsey refers to when he cites long-term track records. I looked at one of their growth funds and a growth and income fund. Both funds owned 22 (of the top 45 holdings) of the same stocks. In other words, if you invested in each of these two funds, you owned many of the same stocks in both portfolios. This is not diversification; it's duplication.

> Maximum diversification, minimal cost, and maximum tax efficiency, low turnover and low turnover cost, and no sales loads.
>
> — JACK BOGLE ON HOW VANGUARD
> ACHIEVED SUCCESS

Bogle's advice is just about the opposite of what Ramsey recommends. Dave's advice is indefensible. It will eventually get you into big trouble, and it's just plain foolish.

> "Focus on long-term returns—ten years or longer if possible."
>
> — DAVERAMSEY.COM.

Really? According to research done by the *Financial Analyst's Journal*,[56] only 6.9% of the nearly 3,000 mutual funds that had been

---

56 2014, "The Career Paths of Mutual Fund Managers: The Role of Merit," By Gary Porter and Jack Trifts

around long enough to be included in their study had managers with at least ten years of experience.

Their research resulted in a couple of enlightening conclusions:

1. "In any given year, even the longest surviving solo managers are unlikely to produce significantly more positive style-adjusted monthly returns than negative ones." The point? Managers with ten years' tenure do not necessarily provide enhanced returns.
2. "The key to a long career in the mutual fund industry seems to be related more to avoiding underperformance than to achieving superior performance." The point? Mediocre investment returns are the norm.

One last jab: according to Morningstar, as many as one out of three mutual fund managers change jobs in any given year. The point? You find the perfect fund for you and your family, only to find out your manager leaves their job in a year or two. Now what? Start all over again? Good luck!

Here is the final nail in the coffin: Dave says, "Focus on long- term returns—ten years or longer if possible." The problem with this advice is that, according to the Schwab Center for Financial Research, "It is hard for active managers to repeat success year after year." Not a single actively managed mutual fund manager ended up in the top-performing quartile[57] every year when at the helm for at least eight years. Got that? Not a single equity mutual fund manager ranked in the top performance quartile for more than seven years in a row.

Under the cost section on how to choose the right mutual funds on DaveRamsey.com, Dave recommends front-end load MFs. He also

---

says, "Pay attention to the fund's expense ratio; a ratio higher than 1% is considered expensive."

What about the rest of the fees mutual funds charge? Transaction or trading costs (approximately 1.44% per year), cash drag, and taxes can also be expensive. According to *Forbes* magazine, the real cost of owning a mutual fund is 3.17% a year in a tax-deferred account like a 401(k) or IRA and a staggering 4.17% per year in a taxable account (including sales charges and commissions). Why Ramsey wants you to pay a 4 to 5% up-front sales charge (which means only 95 to 96% of your money actually gets invested) is beyond my comprehension.

Fees, charges, commissions, and a lack of diversification can destroy your nest egg. Why not invest in an index fund that charges only 0.09% per annum? By doing so, you would save about 3% per year. That would give you an extra $109K in a $100,000 portfolio over a 25-year period. Dave Ramsey's advice is very costly and not very well-thought-out.

And now, the *coup de grâce*:

> "Dave does not recommend exchange-traded funds (ETFs), single stocks, certificates of deposits (CDs), bonds, fixed annuities, variable annuities (VAs), real estate investment trusts (REITs), cash value or whole life insurance."
>
> — DAVERAMSEY.COM

I agree with Dave on the last item. For the most part, life insurance is a terrible place to put your investment dollars. In most policies, the insurance company keeps the cash value or savings and investment portion when the insured passes away. Anyone who thinks that's a good deal needs to have their head examined. I also agree with Dave on CDs; they are savings vehicles, not investments. CDs are ideal for short-term

safe dollars and for an emergency fund. On the other hand, if I agreed
with Dave on the rest of what he "does not recommend," we would both
be wrong.

Let's briefly examine the remaining asset classes Dave does *not*
recommend. First, exchange-traded funds, or ETFs. ETFs, for the
most part, track indexes like the S&P 500. Since the S&P 500 has
outperformed about 90% of all actively managed mutual funds, ETFs
do not have a front-end sales charge, and the internal fees ETFs charge
versus a mutual fund are minuscule, with lower turnover and taxes than
mutual funds, Ramsey's prohibition of ETFs makes no sense.

For whatever reason, single stocks are also forbidden. Hmm—what
about Berkshire Hathaway, a single stock run by Warren Buffett and
(before his passing in 2023) Charlie Munger? These two guys are
arguably the greatest investors of all time. They managed assets of
around one trillion dollars. Compare that with the average mutual fund
with about 20 billion in assets.

Buffett and Munger had a 20% average annual return[58] since 1965
versus 9.9% for the S&P 500 Index. I challenge Dave to find a mutual
fund with a better track record. There aren't any that even come close.
I can think of numerous other individual stocks besides Berkshire
Hathaway that would make suitable investments for a lot of people
seeking growth and/or income. Once again, Dave's advice is baffling.
And just when you thought his judgment could not get any worse, he
surprises us.

Next on Ramsey's forbidden list is bonds. I took the time to listen to
Dave's explanation of why he doesn't recommend bonds on YouTube.
Parenthetically, after watching the video, I would say Dave Ramsey and
I have the perfect face for radio since neither of us is telegenic. He

---

58 Source: Berkshire Hathaway Annual Report 2017

said, "They[59] don't perform as well as stocks over time." That's neither true, factual, or correct. Reality check: the Bloomberg US Aggregate Bond index outperformed the S&P 500 11 out of 42 years (1980–2021). Avoiding the facts does not change them, Mr. Ramsey. You cannot ignore the truth for the sake of convenience; sometimes, bonds do outperform stocks. Period.

What fantasy land does Dave live in? What about the risk mitigation, quarterly income, and diversification bonds provide?

Here's some food for thought: I don't like broccoli. That doesn't mean you shouldn't eat it if you like it, and it is good for you. Just because Mr. Ramsey doesn't like bonds doesn't mean they are not suitable for a lot of folks.

Take 2002, for example. Bonds[60] were up 10.26% for the year, while the stock market[61] was down 22.1%—a 32.36% difference! In 2008, bonds were up 5.24%, while the entire financial system was going into cardiac arrest, and the stock market lost 37%, a 42.24% difference! Bonds can look pretty attractive when the stock market is getting pummeled, don't you think? What about the steady, reliable income stream bonds offer? I'd rather rely on my bond income when the market is down than be forced to sell shares of my "good growth stock mutual funds" at a substantial discount to supplement my income.

I was puzzled when Dave said it was all right to invest in a balanced fund if you want to take on less risk. I am baffled because a typical balanced fund will generally have 30 to 50% of its portfolio invested in bonds. So, why is it not OK to invest in bonds but permissible to invest in a mutual fund with as much as 50% of its holdings in bonds? What

59 Bonds
60 The Balance March 5, 2022
61 The S&P 500

kind of double-talk nonsense is that? Sadly, some people avoid reason until they have tried everything else.

The next asset class not allowed in Ramsey Land is fixed annuities. Dave says fixed annuities are "designed to deliver a guaranteed income for a certain number of years in retirement." Sounds good to me. As a retiree living off my investment and annuity income, I don't see anything wrong with a guaranteed lifetime income stream; it actually comes in pretty handy.

I love the next line from DaveRamsey.com: "Dave doesn't recommend annuities because they are often expensive and charge penalties if you need to access your money during a defined surrender period." OK, Dave—why not buy a no-load annuity with no surrender charges? Problem solved.

Variable annuities (VAs) are next on Dave's no-no list. DaveRamsey.com says: "VAs are insurance products that can provide a guaranteed income stream and death benefit." So, if you don't need a guaranteed income stream and you are not going to die, don't buy a VA. Another problem solved.

On the flip side, however, many retirees find these benefits attractive. Dave goes on to say: "Fees can be expensive, and VAs also carry surrender charges." Yes, indeed, VAs can be expensive, but so are many mutual funds. Why buy a costly VA when you can buy a no-load, no surrender charge variable annuity? I think I already solved that problem above.

Real estate investment trusts (REITs) are also banned in Ramsey Land, even though Dave says they are "similar to mutual funds." So, apparently, it's OK to own mutual funds but not REITs, even though they are similar to mutual funds. I'm not quite sure that makes sense. Here's the best part: "Dave prefers to invest in paid-for real estate bought with cash and does not own any REITs." I'm happy for Dave. He has a net worth of 200 million. So, he can pretty much afford to pay cash for his real estate investments or anything else, for that matter. But what about the rest of us *homo sapiens* who don't have millions lying around?

For the average investor, REITs can make a lot of sense. With a single small investment (like an MF), you can buy a portion of dozens of different properties in various geographical locations and industries (see Chapter 5).

One minor detail Ramsey seems to have overlooked: equity REITs have historically outperformed direct real estate investing,[62] not to mention providing a diversified pool of liquid real estate assets that pay a quarterly dividend and the potential for price appreciation. Even better, REITs are passive investments. You don't have to fix broken stuff.

I'm sitting here pondering Ramsey's logic (or lack thereof). It's OK to buy stock mutual funds, but it's not OK to buy REITs, which are stock mutual funds? Is it permissible or prohibited to buy a stock mutual fund that owns nothing but real estate? While you ponder the question, let me point out that REITs are one of the top-performing asset classes, with a double-digit average annual return over the past 25 years.[63] Why wouldn't you want a top-performing asset class in your portfolio? Why no REITs, Mr. Ramsey? Based on the facts, I'm stumped. Farewell to reason and logic. He will hopefully embrace the truth someday.

OK, that's enough. I am done wandering amongst innumerable absurdities.

Here's the bottom line in my not-so-humble professional opinion: Dave Ramsey provides less-than-brilliant investment advice. Period! Follow it at your own peril. As I said earlier, prescribing without proper diagnosis is malpractice. Anyone who advocates for the entire American

---

62 Source: Forbes magazine, July 19, 2017

63 Source: NAREIT

population to put 100% of their investable assets in the stock market lacks common sense. Obviously, giving sound investment advice is beyond Dave Ramsey's realm of competency. If he was so smart, he'd know he was wrong.

Finally, Dave completely ignores investor behavior: the tendency most folks have to overreact to both positive and negative developments in the markets. Investors are rarely objective and rational, especially if the stock market is getting trashed.[64] So, many sell at precisely the wrong time and lock in permanent losses. He also ignores the impact of having to withdraw money to live on when the stock market is down over a protracted period (reread the story of my new best friend on pages 31 & 32).

Remember, if you follow Dave's investment philosophy, you're taking advice from someone who filed for bankruptcy. He may be entertaining, but his investment advice can lead to disastrous results. I could go on and on, but I will spare you. I recommend you follow Dave's financial advice and completely ignore his investment philosophy. He is, by his own admission, not an investment professional. It is unlikely you will ever become a great investor by listening to Dave Ramsey.

I would tell Mr. Ramsey: "Don't try to be something you are not, an investment professional." Take the advice of Dirty Harry Callahan: "A man's got to know his limitations."

One last thought on Mr. Dave Ramsey: there are certain things I will not do, like skydive, swim with sharks, attend a Bill Clinton abstinence workshop, enroll in the Donald Trump charm school, or take investment advice from an unlicensed talking head. Ironically, you need a license to fish and drive a car, but not to give investment advice, which I find a bit perplexing. Dave's methods are unsound. Which reminds me of

---

64 An old Wall Street adage.

a story. When I was a single guy, living at home with my father and working in the family business, I found out I would inherit a fortune when my sick father died. I decided I needed a wife whom I could share my fortune with. One evening at an investment club meeting, I spotted the most beautiful woman I had ever seen. Her natural beauty took my breath away. "I may look like an ordinary man," I said to her: "but in just a few months, my father will die, and I will inherit $200 million." Impressed, she took my business card, and *three weeks later, she became my stepmother. :)*

Here's another great story from the Bible on how God multiplies. It's from 1 Kings 17:8-16 (NIV):

> [8]Then the word of the Lord came to him, [9]"Go at once to Zarephath in the region of Sidon and stay there. I have directed a widow there to supply you with food." [10]So he went to Zarephath. When he came to the town gate, a widow was there gathering sticks. He called to her and asked, "Would you bring me a little water in a jar so I may have a drink?" [11]As she was going to get it, he called, "And bring me, please, a piece of bread." [12]"As surely as the Lord your God lives," she replied, "I don't have any bread—only a handful of flour in a jar and a little olive oil in a jug. I am gathering a few sticks to take home and make a meal for myself and my son, that we may eat it—and die." [13]Elijah said to her: "Don't be afraid. Go home and do as you have said. But first, make a small loaf of bread for me from what you have and bring it to me, and then make something for yourself and your son. [14]For this is what the Lord, the God of

Israel, says, 'The jar of flour will not be used up, and the jug of oil will not run dry until the day the Lord sends rain on the land.'" [15]She went away and did as Elijah had told her. So, there was food every day for Elijah and for the woman and her family. [16]For the jar of flour was not used up and the jug of oil did not run dry, in keeping with the word of the Lord spoken by Elijah.

If God can multiply flour and oil, he can certainly multiply what you have. Blessings!

11.
STRATEGIES THAT BEAT THE MARKET

Thus far, I've given you several ideas on how to improve your investment results and beat the overall stock market. Here's a quick refresher:

Low price-to-earnings (P/E) quality stocks outperform high P/E stocks. Specifically, investing in stocks in the lowest P/E quartile of the S&P 500 Index returned about 3% more per year than the overall index, while stocks in the highest P/E quartile fell 2% per year below the index.[65] The bottom line: high quality, low P/E stocks outperform.

Dividend-paying stocks outperformed non-dividend-paying stocks over the past four decades by around 6% per year.

By buying quality stocks with low price-earnings ratios with respectable dividend yields, you now have a blueprint that has beat the market over the past 50 years and with lower risk. Welcome to utopia!

---

65 Source: The Future of Investing by Jeremy Siegel

Quality Stocks

Since there doesn't seem to be a universally accepted definition of quality stocks, I will steal Sir John Templeton's definition because it gives an excellent summation. Mr. Templeton was named the greatest global stock picker of the last century. So, it's fair to say he knows what he is talking about:

Quality is a company strongly entrenched as the sales leader in a growing market. Quality is a company that's the technological leader in a field that depends on technical innovation. Quality is a strong management team with a proven track record. Quality is a well-capitalized company that is among the first in a new market. Quality is a well-known, trusted brand for a high-profit-margin consumer product.

Naturally, you cannot consider these attributes of quality in isolation. A company may be a low-cost producer, for example, but it is not a quality stock if its product line is falling out of favor with customers. Likewise, being the technological leader in a technological field means little without adequate capitalization for expansion and marketing.

Determining the quality of a stock is like reviewing a restaurant. You don't expect it to be 100% perfect, but before it gets three of four stars, you want it to be superior.

The Bloomberg US Spin-off Index has produced a total return of 973% since inception (12/31/2002) versus 342% for the S&P 500 Index through the end of 2019. According to investor.gov, in a "spin-off," a parent company distributes shares of a subsidiary to the parent company's shareholders, and the subsidiary becomes a separate, independent company. For example, in 2015 the board of directors at eBay inc. approved the separation of eBay and PayPal into independent, publicly-traded companies. Get the drift? Spin-offs can be extraordinarily profitable!

Companies that **buy back** large blocks[66] of their shares perform better over time than the main stock indices by 2 to 3% per year.

Stock splits have also managed to beat the market by 12% over the three years following the split.

When **insiders** buy large amounts of their company stock, it's an excellent sign. These companies have managed to outperform the overall market by an average of 7% per year over a half-century.

Revisit Chapter Two for more details on these market beaters.

Now, let's look at four additional winning strategies that have excelled over time:

Dogs of the Dow: As I hope you recall, the Dow Jones Industrial Average (DJIA), or the Dow, is a stock market index that measures the performance of 30 large blue-chip companies in the United States. Although not an entirely new concept, it was widely publicized after the release of Michael B. O'Higgins' book, *Beating the Dow*, in which he coined the phrase "Dogs of the Dow."

Here's how it works:

At the end of a calendar year, select the ten highest dividend-yielding stocks in the Dow Jones Industrial Average. You can find these on the dogsofthedow.com website. Next, on the first trading day of the new year, invest an equal dollar amount in each of these ten highest-yielding stocks. In other words, if you have $10,000, you would invest $1,000 in each.

Hold your Dogs of the Dow portfolio for one full year to avoid short-term capital gains. Repeat the process at the beginning of each

---

66 At least 5%

subsequent new year by updating the top ten high-yielding stocks in the Dow 30. Sell your positions that don't make it to the newly updated list and purchase those you don't already own. Put another way, sell any stock that is no longer one of the top ten yielding stocks in the Dow and replace it with those that are. Make sense?

The Dogs of the Dow (or Dow 10) is regarded as one of the most successful investment strategies of all time. The Dogs of the Dow has earned almost 15% a year on average,[67] better than the Dow and the S&P 500, and it's easy!

The **Dow High 5** also beats the Dow Jones Industrial Average. Simply buy an equal dollar amount of the five highest-yielding stocks in the Dow 30. Do the same as above. Buy them on the first trading day of the year, hold them for a full year, sell those that don't make the list a year later, and buy the new stocks that make it onto the list.

Another market-beating strategy is **The Dow Low 5**.

Step 1: Buy the five lowest-priced stocks of the ten highest-yielding stocks in the Dow in equal dollar amounts on the first trading day of each year.

Step 2: Hold for one full year and then sell your positions that no longer meet the criteria.

Step 3: Go back to Step 1 and repeat the process.

By purchasing the five lowest-priced stocks in the Dow with the highest yields, you'll have the least expensive way to own a portfolio with the highest returns.

All three of these strategies beat the DJIA by as much as 3% per year over an extended period. They are the perfect trifecta:

1. The safety of blue chip stocks

---

67 Through the last decade ending in 2019, according to Barron's

2. Income through high dividends
3. Superior performance over time

Who could ask for more?

Not to be outdone, Jeremy Siegel's book, *The Future of Investing*, outlines a fourth game plan for beating the market.

Similar to the Dogs of the Dow, The S&P 10 is a natural extension to apply to another group of large capitalized stocks like those in the S&P 500 Index.

By buying the ten highest-yielding stocks among the largest 100 companies in the S&P 500 on the first trading day of the year and holding them for a full year, you can get even better results than the Dow 10 based on the past 45-year track record.

Now that's something to write home about, don't you think? All the data you need for this strategy can be googled.

A word or two of caution before you dive in. Even though all four of these winning tactics work extremely well over time, they may be severely impacted by future unknown events, such as a terrorist attack, pandemic, or Martian invasion. In other words, past performance may not be indicative of future results.

I'm sure you can tell by now that I'm a fan of some of the greatest investors of all time—as an investment professional responsible for managing lots of money for hundreds of clients over three decades should be. So, in the following pages, I will share some of the wisdom I gleaned from the brightest minds in finance.

David Dreman is a pioneer in contrarian investing and behavioral finance. Dreman is the author of five books on investing and was a senior columnist for *Forbes*. David is the founder and chairman of Dreman Value Management, LLC.

Here are a few snippets from Mr. Dreman's books on behavioral finance:

Conventional financial theory assumes that all investors are rational. However, in reality, emotions can often lead to irrational investment decisions, creating bubbles and panic. Behavioral finance offers clear explanations where current financial theory often fails to recognize and possibly takes advantage of mistakes both professionals and individual investors make.

To survive in the marketplace, it is essential to avoid being carried away by the current mood of the crowd. The investor must find some means of being able to withstand the tide—a task anything but simple. It is first necessary to understand exactly how these crowd influences affect investment decisions and why they are so powerful. Armed with this knowledge, you can develop strategies that should allow you not only to resist the pull of current opinion, but to take advantage of it.

What we see is that not only do investors go wrong, they go wrong in a systematic and predictable manner—so predictable, in fact, that consistent investment strategies can be built on their mistakes. More than that, we can calculate odds on how well our strategies will work over varying periods, in a similar manner to the gambling casino. These strategies have worked for generations and, I suspect, since the dawn of markets. That is, if human behavior hasn't changed.

Market history directly contradicts our academic friends who theorized that investors were always rational, completely unemotional creatures. Investors continually overestimate the outlook for some investments and underestimate the prospects of others. Often, the euphoria or pessimism goes to extremes.

The key principle is that people are not the rational, omniscient decision-makers that the efficient market believers claim and most investment practitioners believe. Rather, we are constantly pushed or pulled by psychological influences.

Unfortunately, according to the findings of a number of clinical studies, overconfidence seems to be a cognitive bias. In other words, the mind is probably designed to extract as much information as possible from what is available but does not realize that the available information is only a small part of the total necessary to build an accurate forecast in uncertain conditions. Evaluating stocks is no different.

Sir John Templeton is one of the greatest global mutual fund managers ever. Whereas Peter Lynch focused on domestic equities, Templeton's claim to fame was his ability to find bargains in the international stock arena. A Rhodes Scholar and Yale grad, his growth fund was one of the first to invest in Japan in the mid-60s and, subsequently, made a lot of money for its investors.

Templeton's best advice: "When buying stocks, search for bargains among quality stocks."

Here are just a few of the many time-tested Templeton maxims:

The time of maximum pessimism is the best time to buy, and the time of maximum optimism is the best time to sell.

If you search worldwide, you will find more bargains (and better bargains) than by studying only one nation. Also, you gain the safety of diversification.

The time to sell an asset is when you have found a much better bargain to replace it.

Best quotes:

"If you buy an asset for one-half or one-fourth what you think it's worth, there is less risk of it going down than if you paid full value for it."

"The only investors who shouldn't diversify are those who are right one hundred percent of the time."

"There is an old saying that when any company or industry gets on the front page of the newspaper, it's too late to buy it. Why? Because other people have already pushed the price up."

"The investor who says, 'This time is different,' has uttered among the four most costly words in the annals of investing."

Peter Lynch is best known for managing the Fidelity Magellan mutual fund for 13 years, during which time his assets under management grew from $20 million to over $14 billion. Mr. Lynch still holds one of the best track records, with an astonishing average annual return of 29%—nearly double what the S&P 500 Index produced for the same period!

As one of the world's best fund managers, he recommends that investors remain independent and open to new investment ideas, often spotted through observation and experience.

Lynch's secret to success: buy stocks with historically low price-to-earnings (P/E ratio) multiples, avoiding companies with hyper-growth and ignoring market forecasts.

Here are a few of Mr. Lynch's golden rules:

Avoid hot stocks in hot industries. Great companies in cold, non-growth industries are consistent winners.

A stock market decline is as routine as a January blizzard in Colorado. If you're prepared, it can't hurt you. A decline is a great opportunity to pick up the bargains left behind by investors who are fleeing the storm in a panic.

There is always something to worry about. Avoid weekend thinking and ignore the latest dire predictions of newscasters. Sell a stock because the company's fundamentals deteriorate, not because the sky is falling.

Best quotes:

"A hot tip at a dinner party is not a good reason to invest your life savings."

"Wonderful companies become risky investments when people overpay for them."

"You have to know what you own and why you own it. 'This baby is a cinch to go up' doesn't count."

Benjamin Graham is considered one of the best value investors of all time. Author of the decades-long bestseller, *The Intelligent Investor*— the holy grail for value investors—Mr. Graham liked to keep things simple: buy a bucket of cheap stocks at a discount to fair value.

Ben taught one of his most famous students, Warren Buffett, how to become a great investor while teaching at Columbia University.

Here is Ben Graham's original checklist to help you find undervalued stocks:

An earnings-to-price yield of at least twice the AAA bond rate

P/E ratio less than 40% of the highest P/E ratio the stock had over the past five years

A dividend yield of at least 2/3 of the AAA bond yield

Stock price below 2/3 of the tangible book value per share

Stock price below 2/3 of the **Net Current Asset Value** (NCAV)

Total debt less than book value

Current ratio greater than 2

Total debt less than two times NCAV

Earnings growth over the past ten years at least at a 7% annual compound rate

Stability of earnings growth—no more than two declines of 5% or more in year-end earnings in the prior ten years are permissible.

Yes, I know the list can look a little intimidating, but fear not. Just google Benjamin Graham stock screener and visit one of the websites that will do the research for you. You're welcome!

Warren Buffett is extensively regarded as one of the most successful stock investors in the world. He is worth about $100 billion USD, which makes him one of the richest people on the planet.

Buffett is the chairman and CEO of Berkshire Hathaway, Inc., an American holding company that serves as an investment vehicle.

The following comparison[68] shows how rich you would be if you were blessed enough to have invested with Mr. Buffett when he started Berkshire Hathaway.

Berkshire Hathaway vs. The S&P 500

Cumulatively since 1965 (including dividends), the S&P 500 has gained 24,708%. If all you had done 58 years ago was invest $10,000 in an S&P 500 index fund, you would have about $2.4 million today. Nearly 60 years is more time than most people have to build a retirement fund, but it gives you an idea of the power of compounding over time.

As incredible as it sounds, if you'd invested in Berkshire Hathaway in 1965, you would have much more money. Since then, Berkshire Hathaway stock has gained 3,787,464%, or more than 153 times the S&P 500's gains over the same period—good enough to give you roughly $355 million based on a $10,000 investment. That translates to a compounded annual gain of 19.8% (nearly double the S&P 500's 9.9% compound annual gain).

Here are Warren Buffett's "Top Three Mistakes to Avoid":

---

68 Source: Nasdaq.com

Trying to time the market. Buffett says, "People that think they can predict the short-term movement of the stock market—or listen to other people who talk about (timing the market)—are making a big mistake."

Trying to mimic high-frequency traders. "Buying stock in a good business and hanging on for the long term," he says, "is a better strategy than flipping stocks like a short-order cook flips pancakes. If they are trading actively, they are making a big mistake," Buffett says.

Paying too much in fees and expenses. "There's no reason to pay an expensive management fee to invest in a mutual fund when super-low-cost index funds that mimic large indexes like the Standard & Poor's 500-stock index are available," he says. "You don't need to look at the prices of the stocks you own from week-to-week, or month-to-month, or even year-to-year," says Buffett. "If you own a cross-section of American businesses, and you don't get excited (and buy) just at the very top, and if you buy in over time, you are going to do well."

Here are three things you should retain from Mr. Buffett:

Buy quality companies at bargain prices.

Quality companies:

Have honest management teams that candidly communicate with shareholders and always act with the interests of shareholders in mind.

Earn more cash than is necessary to stay in business and direct that cash wisely. They either invest in activities that

earn more than they cost or return the cash to shareholders in the form of increased dividends or stock buybacks.
Have high net profit margins.
Increase their market value by more than the value of earnings they retain.

Determine bargain prices by comparing a company's value to its stock price. Buy when the stock is considerably lower than the company's value. This is a straightforward use of Graham's margin of safety.

Focus your portfolio on a few good companies. Concentrating on good stocks is safer than diversifying across mediocre ones.

Just as a business puts more money into its most successful ventures, you should invest more money in your stocks that are performing well.

Do your research, do it well, and disregard the opinions of others.

Warren Buffett is also known as a patient opportunist, waiting for bargains to present themselves. Berkshire was sitting on $128 billion in cash at the end of 2022. For what, you ask? To buy low, I answer—because that's what we are all supposed to do!

Never forget that one of the keys to becoming a Wall Street guru is to use proven strategies like these. You should also be very aware that there are also hundreds of strategies for underperforming the indices. Most have to do with investor foolishness, ignorance,[69] and imprudence.

Since *prudence* is a word rarely used in the English lexicon these days, let's look at the definition:[70]

1. The ability to govern and discipline oneself using reason
2. Sagacity or shrewdness in the management of affairs
3. Skill and sound judgment in the use of resources
4. Caution or circumspection as to the danger of risk

I'm as serious as a funeral right now; you must always be prudent when investing to obtain superior results consistently. A shortage of prudence is a red flag all investors need to recognize in themselves. Investing is not a game, hobby, or thrill-seeking trip to Vegas. As Michael Corleone said, "It's strictly business." Focus on what's important and knowable. Know your limitations; the investment world will eat you alive when you "dabble" in the stock market. During periods of delirious speculation and forgetfulness when you're getting ready to commit financial suicide—stop. Don't drink the Kool-Aid. Check your emotions, turn off the news and financial networks, take a deep breath, and remember that this, too, shall pass. Prudence beats panic! Here's my definition of prudence: loss prevention.

---

69 I'm not trying to be offensive. Will Rogers said, "Everyone is ignorant, only on different subjects."

70 By Merriam-Webster

I'll remind you once more to be careful who you listen to. George Armstrong Custer graduated last—dead last—from the West Point Military Academy. So, be very cautious about who you follow. Foolishness carries a steep price on Wall Street. Understand? Exercise extreme fortitude—be prudent!

> The less prudence with which others conduct their affairs, the greater the prudence with which we should conduct our own affairs.
> — WARREN BUFFETT

Believe it or not, there's a prudent man rule based on common law from the 1830 Massachusetts court. It reads: "To observe how men of prudence, discretion, and intelligence manage their own affairs, not in regard to speculation, but in regard to the permanent disputation of their funds, considering the probable income, as well as the probable safety of the capital to be invested."

I sincerely hope you're getting the point: Avoid imprudence at all costs.

Okay, it's time for something a little more lighthearted than a funeral. Here's a great true story about the Beatles. Yes, I'm a fan, and one of my favorite Beatles songs is "Dear Prudence"—honest. One of the lyrics says: "Dear Prudence, won't you open up your eyes?"

The backdrop to the story is quite interesting. As it turns out, "Prudence" is Prudence Farrow, Mia Farrow's sister and Maureen O'Sullivan's daughter. Yes, that Maureen O'Sullivan of "me Tarzan, you Jane" fame. While Mia and Prudence were studying meditation in India, the Beatles joined the group. Prudence Farrow was preoccupied with meditating in her room for long hours at a time—so much so that her devotion and single-mindedness inspired John Lennon to compose "Dear Prudence."

Ok, back to the funeration. My question for you is: "Won't you open up your eyes" to see the realities necessary for successful and profitable investing?

After all, "It's the business we've chosen," said Hyman Roth.[71]

In closing, I would like to share a short story from my small group, "How to Be a Great Investor", I taught a couple of years ago at my church.

As we were winding down the last class, I asked the group for questions, comments, and feedback. Bob, who was very engaged in the class, asked the following question: "You told us about what you did right over your career. What about some of the investment decisions that did not go so well?"

I pondered Bob's question for a couple of minutes before responding. I had to do a fair amount of soul-searching before I gave him a completely candid answer: "It's what we didn't do that was just as important as what we did do."

For example, we never got caught up in the dotcom (AKA dot bomb) bubble from 1998 to 2000, even though it was very tempting. The fundamentals never made sense with PE ratios as high as 200. So, we exercised **prudence** and avoided a 76.81% plunge in the NASDAQ from 2000 to 2002.

Second, we **never panicked**. When events like the Great Recession of 2007–2009 and COVID-19 hit, we did what we had to do and successfully navigated through the storms by taking advantage of new buying opportunities and changes in the economy. Revisit Chapter 2 and reread the Metropolitain and Prudential stories.

---

71 From *The Godfather II*

We never invested our clients' money in things we did not fully understand—Enron, collateralized mortgage obligations (CMOs), and crypto/bitcoin being the top three endeavors we stayed away from. There is no doubt people made money initially in all of these ventures, but most did not over time. It's speculation and gambling, not investing.

Don't get me wrong; there were unexpected disturbances in the force where our clients experienced temporary short-term declines in their portfolios. But these declines also created incredible buying opportunities for our investors to take advantage of.

As an investment firm, we always did our homework and did our very best to stay on top of our game.

There are many components to success. These chapters have given you many integral ingredients to your own investment success. Use them wisely.

I was walking the beach in Southwest Florida the other day—what was left of it after Hurricane Ian did its damage.

I found myself starting to pray.

I asked God, "How long is a million years to you?"

He said, "Oh, about a second."

I went on to ask him a second question:

"How much is a million dollars to you?"

He responded, "Oh, about a penny."

"Wow!" I exclaimed. "Would you give me a million dollars?"

Without hesitation, God responded, "Sure—in a second."

12.
LIVE LONG AND PROSPER

Yes, I am a Star Trek fan. I was intrigued by the memorable scene from *Star Trek Into Darkness*, when Leonard Nimoy's character, Spock, advises the younger Spock (played by Zachary Quinto) on how to defeat the treacherous villain, Khan. It's a time warp, science fiction moment that gets you thinking. What would I say to a younger me if I could go back in time? Since this book is about investing, and I am a retired investment professional, I'll stick to investment advice for the younger me.

So, what exactly would I say to 25-year-old Richard Everett to help him become a great investor? What wisdom would someone with 35 years of experience impart to a young, uninitiated, new investor? I've thought long and hard before writing this chapter. I waited a couple of weeks for inspiration on how I would end this treatise. I find taking time to think always pays off. I do my best thinking while walking, showering after a workout, or after midday naps (a daily requirement at my age). Many times, I'll go to sleep mulling over a problem, and the solution comes to me as I wake up. My wife, on the other hand, wakes up with the same problem she goes to bed with every night—me! So, the first thing I would tell my young apprentice is that to be a great investor, he must learn to think for himself—to think independently of what others believe or say. Don't listen to the crap on the financial networks. Thinking, for a change, will help him make logical investment decisions.

> Thinking is the hardest work there is, which is probably
> the reason why so few engage in it.
> — HENRY FORD

> It's amazing what you can achieve when you get away
> and intentionally think.
> — JOSEPH P. KENNEDY SR.

Too many people make stupid, emotional investment choices—and end up paying dearly.

Besides focused, unbiased thinking, I would tell the handsome young man walking in my shoes to keep it simple. Successful investing doesn't have to be complicated. Despite what the academics say and the computerized algorithmic models predict, investing, like losing weight, can be pretty simple. Burn more calories than you ingest—exercise more, eat less. Simple? Yes. Easy? No. If you have the basics down, that's all you need to get the job done. Once again, let us return to the wisdom of Warren Buffett:

> Value investing is so simple that it makes people reluctant
> to teach it. If you've gone and gotten a Ph.D. and spent

> several years learning tough mathematics, to have to
> come back to this is like studying for the priesthood and
> then finding out that the Ten Commandments were all
> you needed.

In addition to taking time to think clearly and not overcomplicate the investment process, I would tell the young, debonair Richard to take advantage of his employer's retirement plan. Whether it's a 401(k) or 403(b), he should make sure he signs up to contribute as soon as he is eligible.

There are several good reasons to make this a priority:

1. His contributions to the plan are tax-deductible. That decreases his taxable income. Therefore, he pays less income taxes. In this case, less is better.

2. Many employers will match a percentage of what he puts into his account. Some companies match 25% on a dollar, some 50%, and really generous corporations match dollar for dollar, or 100%, up to a certain limit. Never, never, never turn down free money. Let me repeat—*never, never, never turn down free money!*

3. His retirement plan money grows tax-deferred. Richard pays zero taxes on the appreciation until he takes money out of his account or until age 73 when the IRS requires him to withdraw a percentage of his funds.

4. It will make him a millionaire. A 25-year-old contributing $3,000 per year into a retirement plan for 40 years at an assumed 10% rate of return will have $1,596,333.20 to retire on! That's all it takes—$8.22 a day for his working lifetime. That's definitely worth an "If I were you" lecture from Richard the Elder!

If I had a DeLorean Time Machine, I could talk some sense into a younger, clueless me. Having money automatically deducted from his paycheck forces him to systematically buy shares of a stock mutual fund or index fund inside of his retirement plan. By doing so, he can enhance his overall investment return over time. The concept is called **dollar cost averaging**. It's a pretty neat strategy. By investing the same dollar amount each month over a long period, he will take advantage of buying more shares when the stock market is down. For example, if he were adding $100 per month into his 401(k) from 2008 to 2009 when the market was down over 50%, his $100 would have bought twice as many shares in his mutual fund than he was buying prior to the meltdown. Think about it; when the market recovered and went back to where it was a couple of years earlier, the cheap discounted shares he bought would have doubled in value. Get the concept? Even though the market did not increase in value, Richard makes money by buying on dips.

An example is in order. In the table on the next page, notice that in just 24 months, with the mutual fund share price starting and ending at $25 (breaking even), this faithful investor made $385.75 or a 16% return.[72] Not bad, all things considered.

Dollar cost averaging is a great way to take advantage of volatility in his account and buy additional shares when they go on sale. I would also tell the brawny, rugged youngster how to allocate the assets in his retirement plan. I would instruct him to start by putting 100% of his contributions into an S&P 500 Index fund until his account grew to $100,000. Fortunately, almost all retirement plans offer an index fund.

Remember what I said earlier: index funds have outperformed 90% of all actively managed equity funds. So, he might as well stack the deck in his favor and invest in an S&P 500 Index fund. After the intelligent,

72 For illustrative purposes only

Month	Monthly Investment	Share Price	Shares Purchased
1	$100	$25.00	4
2	$100	$24.00	4.17
3	$100	$23.00	4.35
4	$100	$23.00	4.35
5	$100	$22.00	4.55
6	$100	$22.00	4.55
7	$100	$21.00	4.76
8	$100	$21.00	4.76
9	$100	$20.00	5
10	$100	$20.00	5
11	$100	$19.00	5.26
12	$100	$18.00	5.56
13	$100	$19.00	5.26
14	$100	$19.00	5.26
15	$100	$20.00	5
16	$100	$20.00	5
17	$100	$21.00	4.76
18	$100	$22.00	4.55
19	$100	$22.00	4.55
20	$100	$23.00	4.35
21	$100	$23.00	4.35
22	$100	$24.00	4.17
23	$100	$24.00	4.17
24	$100	$25.00	4
Total Amount Invested	$2,400		111.73

Total Shares Purchased 111.73 Xs
$25.00 = $2,785.75

attractive Richard gets to the 100K mark, I would suggest investing 25% of his portfolio and 25% of his future contributions into an international fund, with 75% still going into his index fund. Once his account had risen to a quarter million dollars, I would suggest allocating 25% of his account and 25% of his future contributions into a bond fund. By now, Richard is older, richer, and wiser. His 250K is broadly diversified by having 50% of his money in an index fund made up of 500 of the biggest and best companies in America: some small-cap, mid-cap, and large-cap stocks, some growth stocks, and some value stocks.

No duplication or overlap, just pure, unadulterated diversification. His other half is split between a bond fund and an international stock fund. Once this mature investor gets closer to retirement (say three to five years out), he should seek advice from a well-seasoned investment professional. Richard will need guidance from someone who is qualified to get him ready for retirement and help navigate him through his retirement years. It's cheaper for him to hire a professional than to become one, especially when it comes to allocating his life savings. There are no second chances in the investment arena. If he makes a major mistake with his nest egg, his retirement funds could become toast.[73]

I would strongly encourage the older, balding, overweight Richard not to go it alone with his million or two at this stage of his life. He's worked too hard and too long to blow it now. Imagine retiring a month or two before a 40 to 50% market decline and watching in horror as his 401(k) shrinks by one-half. I know Richard pretty well. To say he would not be very happy would be a gross understatement. I also know he is not a do-it-yourselfer. One of his favorite sayings is: "If at first you don't succeed—don't try parachuting." I don't think any sane person would risk their lifetime savings by not getting professional investment

---

73 Another Wall Street technical term

advice at this critical point in life. By the way, if Richard's employer didn't offer a retirement plan, I would encourage him to open and fund a Roth[74] IRA in an equity mutual fund or index fund. He should set up an automatic monthly deduction from his checking or savings account. By doing so, he can accumulate a large sum of money tax-free. Remember my "free is good" motto, especially tax-free.

What other investment advice would I give to a youthful Mr. Everett?

Learn from your mistakes and make the necessary adjustments. You don't have to beat yourself up—everyone makes regrettable investment decisions. You're not alone; get over it. Move on—don't let it get you down. Remember, even in Disneyland, only one of the seven dwarfs is Happy!

1. Accept your fallibility. Not all investment decisions will work out. A 70% success rate is outstanding. In baseball, get a hit one out of every three at bats and you could get a 20-million-dollar-a-year contract.

2. Seek opportunities, not guarantees. Buying a quality investment when the price is attractive will almost always turn out to be a home run. On the other hand, most guaranteed investments, such as savings accounts, CDs, and U.S. Treasuries won't make you much money over time after inflation and taxes.

3. Risk is inevitable. No matter how good an investment might look, there will always be risk. Unfortunately, risk is often hidden until it's too late to do anything about it.

---

74 A Roth IRA is an individual retirement account that allows a person to set aside after-tax income each year. The earnings are tax-free after age 59½.

4. The future is a secret—you cannot be certain of anything. Keep that in mind when listening to 'experts' making predictions. Know that you cannot know the unknowable.

5. Volatility is a gift. When the markets go nuts, don't have a nervous breakdown—look for opportunities instead.

6. Avoid being carried away by the current mood of the crowd. Keep your emotions in check. Reason must always overcome feelings.

> Logic is the beginning of wisdom.
> — Spock

7. We shouldn't get hung up on how things *should* be. If we do, we will miss out on how they are. Be flexible and quick to react to change.

> All is flux, nothing stays still, and nothing endures except change.
> — Heraclitus

8. The idea of normal does not exist on Wall Street. Anomalies are regular occurrences.[75] Take advantage of them when they present themselves.

9. Never stop learning. Read books written by successful investors, not theorists.

> Learning from other people's mistakes is much more pleasant.
> — Charlie Munger

---

75 A Wall Street oxymoron

I would also strongly encourage Rich to live below his means, not within his means. I received this advice from one of the richest men in the world many years ago. It served him well, and I am confident it will help Richie stay out of debt.

Social Security and a well-funded 401(k) may not be enough for Richard and his wife to retire on. If either or both live well into their 90s or longer, they could outlive their money. It's hard to be exact when planning for retirement since most folks don't know their dates of death. So, my counsel to this adorable couple is you can't save too much money because you don't know for sure what retirement will truly cost and how long you'll live. Said another way, the cost of saving too little is far greater than the cost of saving too much. They can always give away what's left when they die. On the other hand, it's not likely any bank will lend them money at age 80 so they can continue to live comfortably if they don't save enough.

At least for me, retirement was overrated. I took 2½ years off after selling my investment firm at age 55 so I could do whatever I wanted to do and not be tied down to a career. At first, the time off was both refreshing and invigorating after working long and hard on Wall Street for so many years. But after 30 months, boredom set in. I now keep busy and productive by teaching investment courses at my church and local university. I love to read (about 50 books a year) and write when I can find the time. Keeping my mind active is extremely important at my age. I went to a Ringo Starr concert; he still sounds good for an 83-year-old Beatle! He is the world's richest drummer, worth $350 million. So, why does he still perform? It's certainly not for the money; it's because he loves what he does and wants to stay active. If not, according to Ringo, he'd sleep all day. Being financially independent allows me to help others in need. I'm crazy enough to have gone to Haiti after the devastating

2010 earthquake to lend a hand. I've also made several trips to Rwanda after the genocide. If spending time in either of these countries doesn't put someone's life into perspective, nothing will. Being able to bless my children and grandchildren is an awesome feeling, too. My point is that the young Mr. Everett can't help others unless he has it to give away. Being a great investor can help make it possible! He must take the time to learn how to become a great investor so he and his wife can have an abundant life, retire comfortably, help folks in need, and leave a legacy for his children and grandchildren.

It's an awesome feeling to be able to give to his church and missionaries. To help build schools, Bible colleges, medical clinics, dig wells, help free women caught up in sexual slavery, and change the world for the better. It's an amazing privilege to be part of the solution.

Don't miss this. It's far better to have his money work for him rather than to have him work for his money. To do so, he must learn how to become a great investor.

So, young Mr. Everett, in closing, I leave you with a final thought from Sarek, Mr. Spock's father: "You are fully capable of deciding your own destiny. The question you face is: Which path will you choose? That is something only you can decide. Choose wisely." No wouldas, shouldas, or couldas, and no regrets.

I've shared several examples from the Bible throughout this book on how our God is in the multiplication business. If He can multiply loaves, fish, oil, and flour, He can surely multiply the "talents" or resources He has given you. God admonishes us in Genesis 1:28 to "be fruitful and multiply."

The phrase "to be fruitful" means to be productive. The word "multiply" means to increase in number. God is not suggesting; He is making a very strong exhortation. We are to be in the multiplication business! By becoming great investors, we will someday hear the words of our master saying: "Well done, good and faithful servant! You have been faithful with a few things; I will put you in charge of many things. Come and share your master's happiness!"

May you live as long as you want and never want as long as you live. May you live long and prosper.

May you always be blessed!

R. Everett

EPILOGUE

You know it's a bad day when today's stock market report looks like this (one final attempt at humor):

Helium was up. Feathers were down. Paper was stationary.

Fluorescent tubing was dimmed in light trading. Knives were up sharply.

Cows steered into a bull market. Pencils lost a few points. Hiking equipment was trailing.

Elevators rose while escalators continued their slow decline. Weights were up in heavy trading.

Mining equipment hit rock bottom. Diapers remain unchanged. Shipping lines stayed at an even keel.

The market for raisins dried up. Coca-Cola fizzled.

Caterpillar stock inched up a bit. Sun peaked at midday.

Balloon prices were inflated.

Scott tissue touched a new bottom.

> But remember the Lord your God, for it is He who gives you the ability to produce wealth.
> — DEUTERONOMY 8:18 (NIV)

Let the Lord be magnified who hath pleasure in the prosperity of His servant.

   — PSALM 35:27 (NKJV)

APPENDIX A: WHAT YOU SHOULD RETAIN FROM THIS BOOK

I have provided several proven investment strategies throughout this book to help you beat the market. They can all help you invest like a pro and enhance your returns over time. Achieving superior investment returns may be challenging, but it doesn't have to be overly complicated.

As a certified investment geek, I urge you to follow the steps I have laid out in these chapters and profit from them! Investing nirvana awaits. Just "follow the yellow brick road."

Chapter 1: If Only Investing Were Easy

1. If you buy smart and remain patient, you will do well in the long run.
2. Avoid predictions; stick with the known facts.
3. Geniuses are not better investors than anyone else.

Chapter 2: Stocks and the Stock Market

Your success or failure is directly proportional to the price you pay.

Dividends matter a lot.

Are insiders buying or selling?

Chapter 3: Let's Do Some Bonding

Bonds can be relatively safe.

Bonds provide predictable income and risk mitigation.

Bonds are interest-rate sensitive. Be careful when you buy.

Chapter 4: Mutual Funds and Exchange-Traded Funds

Mutual funds make money in three ways: income earned from dividends and bonds, capital gains, and capital appreciation.

Mutual funds can have high fees and generate a lot of taxes. Always do your homework. By doing so, you can save a bundle.

Exchange-traded funds are tax-efficient and have very low fees.

Chapter 5: Real Estate Investment Trusts

REITs are an efficient way to diversify your portfolio.

REIT dividends are generally taxed at a lower rate than ordinary income.

Over the long term, REITs have outperformed the major market indices.

Chapter 6: Annuities

Some are good—some are bad.

Annuities can provide a guaranteed income stream for life.

The average fixed index annuity return during the Great Depression would have been 6.4%.

Chapter 7: How to Construct a Portfolio That is Right for You

All investments have some level of risk.

You're absolutely crazy if you don't diversify.

Just about every investment professional agrees you should rebalance your portfolio regularly.

Chapter 8: Getting Sound Investment Advice

Anyone who sells investment products for a commission is not your friend.

Anyone can call themselves a financial planner—the title is meaningless.

Registered Investment Advisors are fiduciaries and are held to a higher standard by the U.S. Securities and Exchange Commission (SEC).

Chapter 9: Behave Yourself

Studies confirm that most individuals are lousy investors.

Most individual investors act irrationally.

Fear and greed are an investor's worst enemy.

Chapter 11: Strategies that Beat the Market

The Dogs of the Dow outperforms the Dow Jones Industrial Average over time.

The S&P 10 performs even better.

Prudence is a virtue.

Chapter 12: Live Long and Prosper

Think for a change.

Take advantage of free money.

Dollar-cost averaging is a moneymaking machine in a retirement plan with a long-term time horizon.

APPENDIX B:
THE WALL STREET ZOO

Black Swans

A *black swan* event comes as a negative or positive surprise that was completely unexpected when it occurred. The term originated from the belief that all swans were white because they were the only ones known in the West until Dutch explorers discovered black swans in Australia in 1697.

A Dog with Fleas

This saying points to a defect in a company, but a dog with fleas can go to a vet and be treated. So, an underperforming stock may be attractive once they fix their problems—assuming they are fixable.

Unicorns

Fast-growing, privately held companies waiting for favorable market conditions to go public via an IPO.

A Red Herring

A *red herring* is a preliminary prospectus filed by a company with the Securities and Exchange Commission in connection with the company's IPO.

Dead Cat Bounce

A *dead cat bounce* happens after an individual stock or the entire stock market has dropped; there is often a temporary upward bounce until the decline continues.

Pigs

Pigs are greedy and impatient. They invest in tips and emotions. They eventually get slaughtered.

Bulls

Individual investors that are optimistic that the stock market will increase in the short term.

Bears

Individual investors that are pessimistic about the market in the short term.

Wolves

Wolves make money either unethically or illegally. They eventually go to jail and share a cell with Bernie Madoff.

Bottom Fishing

Bottom fishing refers to buying a stock that has experienced a decline and may be undervalued.

Dogs of the Dow

An investment strategy that buys the ten highest-yielding stocks in the Dow Jones Industrial Average in approximately equal dollar amounts on the first trading day of each year and holds them for one full year. Once the new year begins, the process is repeated.

APPENDIX C: READING LIST

I highly recommend the following books on investing. They are all current and relevant, full of insight and wisdom from some of the greatest minds in the investment world. You will notice there are no books by Peter Lynch, John Templeton, or Warren Buffett. Both Lynch's and Templeton's books are somewhat dated, and Buffett has yet to write a book. You can, however, read his annual letters dating back to 1977 free of charge on the berkshirehathaway.com website. The shareholder letters are priceless.

The Most Important Thing by Howard Marks
> By far, my favorite book on investing.

Mastering the Market Cycle by Howard Marks
> A great read on how to stack the odds in your favor.

Bogle on Mutual Funds by John C. Bogle
> Jack is the founder of the Vanguard Group and champion of index fund investing.

Stock for the Long by Jeremy J. Siegel
> The book contains an amazing amount of research and data.

The Future for Investors by Jeremy J. Siegel
> I really enjoyed this book and learned a great deal. My biggest takeaway was that I didn't know everything.

And finally, I would suggest three of Joel Greenblat's books. Joel is a wealth of knowledge and sagacity:

You Can be a Stock Market Genius
The Little Book That Still Beats the Market
The Big Secret for the Small Investor

Financial Websites

Use these sites for information, data, and news—not opinions:
CNBC.com
GreatInvestor.org
FOXBusiness.com
MarketWatch.com
MorningStar.com

Financial Publications

The Wall Street Journal, published six days a week, and *Barron's*, published weekly. I find both to be informative and unbiased publications. Once again, stay away from opinions and stick with the facts.

APPENDIX D
103 QUOTES FROM THE WORLD'S GREATEST INVESTORS A POLITICIAN, A THEORETICAL PHYSICIST, AND MY WIFE

1. "People who habitually purchase common stocks at more than about 20 times their average earnings are likely to lose considerable money in the long run."
   — Graham and Dodd, Authors of *Security Analysis*

2. "A very important ingredient of successful stock investing is courage: the courage to buy when others are selling; the courage to buy when stocks are hitting new lows; the courage to buy when the economy looks bad; courage to buy at the bottom. If you look back over the years, you will note that the times when the gloom was the thickest invariably turned out to have been the best times to buy stocks."
   — Fred J. Young, Author of the best-selling book, *Investment Planning: How to Get Rich and Stay Rich*

3. "In a recent Staff Letter, we discussed the futility of trying to forecast the immediate trend of stock prices. It must be apparent to intelligent investors that if anyone possessed the ability to do so consistently and accurately, he would become a billionaire so quickly he would not find it necessary to sell his stock market guesses to the general public."

   — David Babson, Founder of David L. Babson & Co., a multibillion-dollar private investment firm

4. "Those who say, don't know, and those who know, don't say."

   — Michael Lewis, best-selling author

5. "If riskier investments could be counted on to produce higher returns, they wouldn't be riskier."

   — Howard Marks, Co-Founder and Co-Chairman of Oaktree Capital Management and author

6. "To have unconventional success, you can't be guided by conventional wisdom."

   — David Swenson, Chief Investment Officer at Yale University and author

7. "There are two kinds of people who lose money: Those who know nothing and those who know everything."

   — Henry Kaufman, President of Henry Kaufman & Company, a financial consulting firm

8. "An economist is an expert who will know tomorrow why things he predicted yesterday didn't happen today."

   — Laurence J. Peter, best known for formulating the *Peter Principle*

9. "If you want to see the greatest threat to your financial future, go home and take a look in the mirror."
    — Jonathan Clements, author of *From Here to Financial Happiness*

10. "Whenever some analyst seems to know what he is talking about, remember that pigs will fly before he'll ever release a full list of his past forecasts, including the bloopers."
    — Jason Zweig, journalist and author

11. "No rule always works. The environment isn't controllable, and circumstances rarely repeat exactly."
    — Howard Marks

12. "If you're not willing to react with equanimity to a market price decline of 50% two or three times a century, you're not fit to be a common shareholder, and you deserve the mediocre result you're going to get compared to the people who do have the temperament, who can be more philosophical about these market fluctuations."
    — Charlie Munger, Vice Chairman of Berkshire Hathaway

13. "A great business at a fair price is superior to a fair business at a great price."
    — Charlie Munger

14. "Whether you invest in individual stocks, an actively managed fund, or an index fund, the sources of your regrets are likely to fall into one of five mistakes:
    1) Allowing emotions, not reason, to guide decisions
    2) Thinking you know more than you actually do
    3) Trusting capital to the wrong people
    4) Choosing businesses prone to failure because of obsolescence competition or excessive debt

5) Overpaying for stocks, most frequently those with vivid, striking stories."

— Joel Tillinghast, Manager of the Fidelity Low-Priced Stock Fund and author

15. "Be skeptical and willing to challenge ideas others take for granted. Everyone needs a crap detector."

— Joel Tillinghast

16. "You can't make money from anything millions of viewers have seen on TV or the Internet."

— Joel Tillinghast

17. "Even if your judgment is sound, randomness has a lot of influence on outcomes."

— Howard Marks

18. "Honesty was never a profit center on Wall Street."

— James Grant, writer and publisher

19. "It is the nature of the sound-bite driven media that superficial opinions are preferred to in-depth analysis."

— Robert Shiller, economist, academic, best-selling author, and Nobel Prize winner

20. "As an intellectual matter, stock prices are not forecastable."

— Robert Shiller

21. "When Wall Street gets innovative—watch out!"

— Warren Buffett, Chairman of Berkshire Hathaway

22. "At the point when everyone feels like they want to throw up, that is exactly the point when I might want to look at a company."

— Ramona Persaud, Fidelity Dividend Growth Portfolio Manager

23. "Don't fall in love with an investment—be situation-dependent and opportunity-driven."

— Charlie Munger

24. "It is better to be roughly right than precisely wrong."

    — John Maynard Keynes, economist

25. "Just because a company is doing poorly doesn't mean it can't do worse."

    — Peter Lynch, mutual fund manager and best-selling author

26. "The more you learn, the more you earn."

    — Warren Buffett

27. "Advice from the average investor obviously can't help you be an above-average investor."

    — Howard Marks

28. "Forecasts create the mirage that the future is knowable."

    — Peter Bernstein, financial historian, economist, and educator

29. "Event-driven opportunities exist on a regular basis and can be exploited with superior analytical skills."

    — David Swenson

30. "The market's boundless capacity for poor judgment ensures a steady supply of out-of-favor candidates."

    — John Neff, investor, mutual fund manager, and author

31. "Occasionally, successful investing requires inactivity."

    — Warren Buffett

32. "History provides a crucial insight regarding market crises – they are inevitable, painful, and ultimately surmountable."

    — Shelby Davis, money manager

33. "People overbuy growth stocks. They pay too much for growth stocks. They ignore value stocks. They ignore slow growers. They tend to be underpriced. Therefore, over the long run, you are going to get a better return."

    — Jeremy Siegel, Professor of Finance at the Wharton School and best-selling author

34. "Markets are not something you predict; markets are something you take advantage of."

— Marty Whitman, portfolio manager and author

35. "Anything that isn't impossible is inevitable."

— Nick Murray, financial writer

36. "Cash combined with courage in a time of crisis is priceless."

— Warren Buffett

37. "When the facts change, I change my mind."

— John Maynard Keynes

38. "To be a notable investor, you should disagree with popular thinking."

— John Train, investment advisor and author

39. "No matter how sophisticated our choices, how good we are at dominating the odds, randomness will have the last word.

— *Fooled by Randomness* by Nassim Nicholas Taleb

40. "Bulls make money, bears make money, and 'pigs' get slaughtered."

— an old Wall Street saying that warns investors against excessive greed

41. "Junk bonds will one day live up to their names."

— Warren Buffett

42. "The riskiest thing is overpaying for an asset (regardless of the quality), and the best way to reduce risk is by paying a price that's irrationally low."

— Howard Marks

43. "Virtually anyone's ability to predict the stock market and economy rounds to zero. The future is unknowable; the economy is highly complicated."

— Bill Miller, investor and fund manager

44. "Not knowing when to sell can obliterate your gains."
— John Neff

45. "Ride the winners and sell the losers."
— Burton G. Malkiel, economist and best-selling author

46. "The idea that trading success is tied to finding some specific ideal approach is misguided. There is no single correct methodology."
— *The Little Book of Market Wizards* by Jack D. Schwager

47. "I know a lot of people would like to say one would have the ability to learn it, but I actually think you cannot. Because it is all those intangibles, it is the passion, it is the humility, it is the intelligence, it is the fortitude, it is all those things packaged into one."
— Jane Siebels on 'Learning the Investment Business'

48. "Success is purely a function of two things: recognition of the inevitability of major market declines; and emotional/behavioral preparation to regard such declines as nonevents."
— Nick Murray

49. "Every investment has something wrong with it."
— Marty Whitman

50. "At a high enough price, even the best companies are highly speculative (Nifty 50), and, at a low enough price, even the worst companies are a sound investment."
— *The Four Pillars of Investing* by William J. Bernstein, financial theorist

51. "What separates the professional from the amateur are two things: First, the knowledge that brutal bear markets are a fact of life and that there is no way to avoid their effects. And second, that when times get tough, the former stays the course; the latter abandons the blueprints, or, more often than not, has no blueprint at all."

— *The Four Pillars of Investing* by William J. Bernstein

52. "Wealth is not determined by investor performance but by investor behavior."

— Nick Murray

53. "Never forget the financial law of gravity."

— Burton G. Malkiel

54. "You know, when I first came to Wall Street, I assumed that everybody knew much more than I did, understood things, and if they said the sky is blue, then there is no reason to look out the window and check. The sky is blue. These are older, smarter, and more successful people...So I came to realize, well, it was mainly that I built some confidence, but more and more, I realized these guys did not have a clue what they were talking about. I would hear them say things that just astonished me, and then I would go the other way. If you do that enough times, and you are right more than they are right, it would make you more confident and more successful."

— Jim Rogers, investor and author

55. "If you begin with prayer, you will think more clearly and make fewer mistakes."

— John Templeton, investor, mutual fund manager, and author

56. "Reality lay somewhere between the extremes of wild enthusiasm and deep despair."

— David Swenson

57. "Investing must be rational; if you don't understand it, don't do it."
— Warren Buffett

58. "As a general rule of thumb, the more complexity that exists in a Wall Street creation, the faster and further investors should run."
— David Swenson

59. "The most painful lesson that was repeatedly hammered home is that you can *never* be sure of anything: There are always risks out there that can hurt you badly, even in the seemingly safest bets, so it's always best to assume you're missing something."
— Ray Dalio, hedge fund manager and best-selling author

60. "Some investors should be cutting flowers in their garden and letting smart people run the money."
— Adam Smith, economist and author

61. "Discount the obvious, bet on the unexpected."
— George Soros, investor and author

62. "After all is said and done, there is no surefire solution for investment success."
— John Bogle, Founder of The Vanguard Group, best-selling author

63. "Don't confuse luck and skill when judging others, and especially when judging yourself."
— Carl Icahn, Founder of Icahn Enterprises

64. "Here we confront the main irony: *One of the most obvious and consistent variables that can be harnessed into a workable investment strategy is the continuous overreaction of man himself to companies he considers to have excellent or mundane prospects. This works just as surely with the investor today as it has with*

investors in all markets of the past."

— David Dreman, Chairman of Dreman Value Management, LLC and author

65. "All great investors and investment approaches have bad patches; losing faith in them at such times is as common a mistake as getting too enamored of them when they do well. Because most people are more emotional than logical, they tend to overreact to short-term results; they give up and sell low when times are bad and buy too high when times are good."

— Ray Dalio

66. "Patient opportunism—waiting for bargains—is often your best strategy. An opportunist buys things because they're offered at bargain prices."

— Howard Marks

67. "The market has good days and bad days, good years and bad years. You can't predict them, and they can reverse course with stunning speed. But you can learn to cope with them and improve your odds."

— John Neff

68. "Patience is a crucial but rare investment commodity."

— David Dreman

69. "Prices fluctuate more than values—so therein lies opportunity."

—Joel Greenblatt, hedge fund manager, academic, and best-selling author

70. "The first rule investors should understand is that what goes up must come down, and what comes down must go up."

— John Bogle

71. "Comfortable investment decisions fail to generate exciting results. Discomfort represents a necessary, albeit not sufficient, condition of success."

    —David Swenson

72. "An investor who has all the answers doesn't even understand the questions."

    —John Templeton

73. "By looking only at the historical numbers, the star system identifies what worked in the past, not what might work in the future. In a market that enjoys sustained rushes of enthusiasm and suffers long-lasting bouts of despair, Morningstar's backward-looking performance measurement metrics prove useless to forward-looking investors. Sensible investors avoid Morningstar's useless ratings."

    — David Swenson

74. "A market crisis presents an outstanding opportunity to profit because it lets loose overreaction at its wildest. Although gut-wrenching, holding—and even buying—in a panic is a winning strategy."

    — David Dreman

75. "It's essential they be aware that they are at a competitive disadvantage in terms of education, experience, and quality of information. It's not a game." (Advice to part-time investors)

    — Michael Steinhardt, investor and hedge fund manager

76. "Buy stocks of growing businesses, managed by people of vision, who understand significant social and economic trends and who are preparing for the future through intelligent R&D."

    — Thomas Rowe Price, Jr., Founder of T. Rowe Price, an American-based investment firm

77. "The panic that gripped many investors had created the finest buying opportunity of the decade."

— David Dreman

78. "There is no wealth in the stock market without risk."

— John Bogle

79. "Abnormally good or abnormally bad conditions do not last forever."

—Benjamin Graham

80. "Experience tends to confirm a long-held notion that being prepared, on a few occasions in a lifetime, to act promptly in scale, in doing some simple and logical thing, will often dramatically improve the financial results of that lifetime. A few major opportunities, clearly recognizable as such, will usually come to one who continuously searches and waits, with a curious mind that loves diagnosis involving multiple variables. And then all that is required is a willingness to bet heavily when the odds are extremely favorable, using resources available as a result of prudence and patience in the past."

— Charlie Munger

81. "Selling your winners and holding your losers is like cutting the flowers and watering the weeds."

— Peter Lynch

82. "Now, information moves so fast that whatever insight you have, a million other people have it, posted it, tweeted about it, and it's already affected the stock."

—Barry Ritholtz, equities analyst, financial blogger, and author

83. "However beautiful the strategy, you should occasionally look at the results."
    —Winston Churchill, former Prime Minister of the United Kingdom

84. "We are value investors because we are persuaded of the logic of buying shares of businesses when others want to sell them, and we understand that lower prices today mean higher future rates of return, and high prices today mean lower future rates of return."
    — Bill Miller

85. "Nobody ever lost money taking a profit."
    — Bernard Baruch, financier, stock investor, statesman, and author

86. "At the end of the day, stock prices move with earnings."
    — Peter Lynch

87. "If you're even a slightly above average investor who spends less than you earn over a lifetime, you cannot help but get very wealthy—if you're patient."
    — Warren Buffett

88. "Should you avoid the stocks the experts or the crowd are pursuing and pursue the ones they are avoiding? The answer is an unqualified 'Yes.'"
    — David Dreman

89. "The market does reflect the available information, as the professors tell us. But just as the funhouse mirrors don't always accurately reflect your weight, the markets don't always accurately reflect that information. Usually, they are too pessimistic when it's bad and too optimistic when it's good."
    — Bill Miller

90. "If insiders don't buy their own stock on recessions, who should? The absence of inside support is generally accepted as a pretty good bear tip."

    —Jesse Livermore, a well-known stock trader from days gone by

91. "The main purpose of the stock market is to make fools of as many men as possible."

    — Bernard Baruch

92. "One of the essential qualifications of the successful investor is patience."

    —Philip Carret, Founder of the Pioneer Fund and author

93. "Wall Street is about telling stories and making predictions—and sadly, people pay a lot for predictions. Our desire to believe a good story when it is more appealing than a solid fact is a basic human flaw."

    — Larry Hite, hedge fund manager and author

94. "If, when making a stock investment, you're not considering holding it for at least ten years, don't waste more than ten minutes considering it."

    — Warren Buffett

95. "To summarize: don't be stubborn, don't be greedy, and don't be afraid to take small losses. Above all, when you buy a stock, make a mental decision as to the level at which you will sell it—and stick to that decision. You may lose a few points at the top, but you'll make a lot more than you'll lose in the long run."

    —David Dreman

96. "It is the nature of financial markets to be subject to sharp price fluctuations, to be buffeted by events, and often to be emotionally trying. Successful investing involves the disciplined and patient execution of a long-term strategy, especially when it is emotionally difficult. That is usually the time the opportunities are the greatest."
— Bill Miller

97. "The chief losses to investors come from the purchase of low-quality securities at times of favorable business conditions."
— Benjamin Graham

98. "Conservative investors sleep well."
— Philip Fisher, investor and best-selling author

99. "There's more than one road to investment heaven."
— Joel Greenblatt

100.   "We are determined, as always, to keep our heads while others seemed intent on losing theirs."
— John Neff

101.   "So, let's be clear: it's not asset quality that determines investment risk. The price of an asset is the principal determinant of its riskiness."
— Howard Marks

102.   "Never fool yourself, and remember that you are the easiest person to fool."
—Richard Feynman, theoretical physicist

103.   "So why do they call them *experts*?"
— MarySue Everett, my wife

APPENDIX E:
INDEX OF BASIC
FINANCIAL TERMS

401(k): Under section 401(k) of the Internal Revenue Code, employees can set aside money for retirement on a pre-tax basis through a plan sponsored by their employer. To encourage saving for retirement through these plans, the federal government created special tax advantages for 401(k) contributions.

Asset Allocation: Asset allocation means spreading your investments over different types of investment categories. By capitalizing on this concept, you can invest some assets for safety, income, and growth.

Asset Class: A group of investments considered similar in potential risk and return. There are three basic asset classes: stocks, bonds, and short-term securities (or cash).

Assets: Assets are the property and resources (such as cash and investments) of a person or company. A mutual fund's assets include whatever securities (stocks, bonds, Treasury bills, etc.) it owns, plus any cash.

Bear Market: A term signifying a decline in the market.

Bid and Ask: The bid is the price for a security or commodity, and the ask is the price requested. The quote (also known as the quotation) is the bid and ask on a security or commodity. For instance, a quote on a given stock may be 20.25 bid and 20.50 asked. In other words, the highest price a buyer wanted to pay was $20.25, and the lowest the seller was willing to take was $20.50.

Blue Chip: A stock that is low-risk because the company has a reputation for reliability, quality, and the ability to make money and pay dividends.

Bonds: Bonds are essentially loans (or debt instruments). They're issued by corporations, governments, or municipalities to raise money. A bond certificate is like an IOU. It shows the amount loaned (principal), the rate of interest to be paid, and the date that the principal will be repaid (maturity date). Mutual funds that invest primarily in bonds are also called "income" funds.

Broker: An agent who has passed a test to determine their basic knowledge in securities, is registered with the S.E.C., and may charge a fee to buy and sell securities, commodities, and real estate to and for the public.

Bull Market: The term used to express a rise in the market.

Common Stocks: When people talk about a company's stock, they usually mean common stock. When you own common stock in a company, you share in its success or failure. As part owner, you vote on important policy issues (such as picking the board of directors). If the company prospers, you may get part of the profits, called dividends. Also, the value of your shares in the company may increase; common stock generally has the most substantial potential for growth but carries the most significant risk since that value can drop if the company does poorly. If the company goes bankrupt, common stockholders are the last to receive proceeds from its liquidation.

Closed-End Fund: "A closed-end fund (or CEF) is an investment company managed by an investment firm. Closed-end funds raise a certain amount of money through an initial public offering (or IPO), after which it can list shares on a stock exchange. Like mutual funds and ETFs, closed-end funds invest in a basket of securities" (Nerd Wallet).

Collateralized Mortgage Obligation (CMO): Wikipedia.com defines a collateralized mortgage obligation (CMO) as "a type of complex debt security that repackages and directs the payments of principal and interest from a collateral pool to different types and maturities of securities, thereby meeting investor needs."

Commodity: A commodity is a raw material (such as an agricultural product), a precious metal (like gold or silver), or an energy resource (such as oil or natural gas).[76]

Compounding: When you put money in the bank, it earns interest. When that interest earns interest, the result is "compound" interest. Compound interest also occurs if bond income (or dividends from stocks or mutual funds) is reinvested into your account. Compounding can help your balance increase expeditiously.

Convertible Bond: Bonds that (at the option of the investor) may be converted into other securities of the underlying corporation. The owner of the convertible bond (you) may find it profitable to exercise their option if the value of the stock into which it is converted subsequently exceeds the value of the bond at the conversion price. Convertible bonds are often attractive because they allow the purchaser the safety of a bond or an increase in value through the conversion option.

---

76 Source: BlackRock.com

Cryptocurrency: Cryptocurrency is an umbrella term for a variety of virtual "currencies" that can be exchanged digitally and anonymously. They are not overseen by any central bank or authority as traditional currencies are. Central to their appeal to those who use them, they are heavily encrypted and decentralized. Responsibility for their administration is spread globally among holders via the Internet.[77]

Debenture: According to Wikipedia.com, "In corporate finance, a debenture is a medium- to long-term debt instrument used by large companies to borrow money at a fixed rate of interest. The legal term "debenture" originally referred to a document that creates a debt or acknowledges it, but in some countries, the term is now used interchangeably with bond, loan stock, or note."

Derivative: "A derivative is a security whose underlying asset dictates its pricing, risk, and basic term structure. Investors use derivatives to hedge a position, increase leverage, or speculate on an asset's movement. Derivatives can be bought or sold over the counter or on an exchange" (Investopedia.com).

Diversification: This concept of spreading your money across various investments could potentially moderate your investment risk. It's the idea of not putting all your eggs in one basket. A diversified portfolio can help shield you from large losses because even if some securities falter, others may perform well.

Dividend: The amount of payment decided by the board of directors to be made to the shareholder for each share held. Preferred shareholders typically receive a fixed amount, which was determined when the preferred share was issued.

---

77 Source: Forbes.com

Dollar Cost Averaging: Money is invested at regular intervals in the same investment. Because you invest the same amount each time, you automatically buy more shares when the price is lower. Though the method doesn't guarantee a profit or guard against loss in declining markets, the average cost of each share is usually lower if you buy over a prolonged period.

Dow Jones Industrial Average: A formula that represents the stock prices of 30 major industrial companies in the United States. Because it includes companies that represent core sectors of our economy, the Dow is considered the most accepted indicator of overall market performance. When the Dow is up, it means the prices of those companies rose collectively during the day; when it's down, they declined.

Equity: This means ownership in a company. When you own shares of a company's stock, you own equity in that company. So, stock investments are also called "equities." Similarly, mutual funds that invest in stocks are often called "equity funds."

Federal Deposit Insurance Corporation (FDIC): The U.S. Government entity that insures deposits in American member banks up to $250,000 per depositor ownership category, per bank. The FDIC was established by the Banking Act of 1933 to reduce bank runs by increasing depositor confidence. Over one-third of banks failed prior to the FDIC's creation during the Great Depression.

Futures: Investopedia.com defines futures as "derivative financial contracts obligating the buyer to purchase an asset at a predetermined future date and set price. A futures contract allows an investor to speculate on the price of a financial instrument or commodity."

Ginnie Mae: A nickname for Government National Mortgage Association. Like modified pass-thru mortgage securities, these are guaranteed by the United States Government.

Inflation: When the price of goods and services rises over time, the result is called inflation. This means that the things you buy today will cost more in the future.

Index/Benchmark: An index measures the price and performance of a specific group of stocks. There are many indexes that an investor can track each business day, including the Dow Jones Industrial Average and the S&P 500.

Inverted Yield Curve: "In finance, an inverted yield curve happens when a yield curve graph of (typically) government bonds inverts and the shorter-term bonds are offering a higher yield than the long-term bonds" (Wikipedia.com).

Investment Mix: The combination of investment options you choose for your portfolio.

Investment Option Types: Each option has its own investment objective based on a targeted level of investment risk and return. There are several types of investment options:

Asset allocation **funds spread their assets over various investment categories, including cash, bonds, and equities (stocks). They gradually adjust this mix of investments as market conditions change.**

Balanced funds **buy a mix of common stocks, preferred stocks, and bonds. Their goal is to blend long-term growth from stocks and income from dividends and bonds.**

Growth funds **invest in the stocks of various types of companies (both foreign and domestic) with the potential to grow.**

Growth and income funds **invest in different types of bonds and stocks of both foreign and domestic companies.**

Income funds **(or "bond funds") purchase various types of bonds with varied maturities and quality.**

International funds **usually invest most of their assets in stocks or bonds of companies and governments outside the United States.**

Investment Risk: The chance that you may lose a portion of your investment principal.

Issuer: A company, government, or municipality that offers bonds to investors. (See Bonds.)

Junk Bond: A bond considered high-risk because of its low rating.

Management Styles: There are two types of management styles:

Active management **means that a portfolio manager is trying to outperform the market. Whatever the market does (as measured by specific benchmarks), the manager will try to do better and increase value for investors.**

Passive management means that a portfolio manager is trying to achieve a return for the inves**tor that is comparable to the return of the overall market or an index.**

Margin Account: A margin account allows you to borrow money from a brokerage firm to buy securities. It's also the only account type in which investors can engage in short selling. In a margin account, you deposit a portion of the purchase price of the security in the account and borrow the rest from the firm.[78]

Morningstar, Inc.: According to Wikipedia, "Morningstar, Inc. is an American financial services firm headquartered in Chicago, Illinois, and was founded by Joe Mansueto in 1984. It provides an array of investment research and investment management services."

NASD: Abbreviation of National Association of Security Dealers, Inc. An organization for brokers and dealers in the over-the-counter securities business.

NASDAQ: Abbreviation of National Association of Securities Dealers Automated Quotations. An electronic system that provides brokers and dealers belonging to NASD with price quotations on securities traded over-the-counter.

No-Load Fund: An investment company that does not make a sales charge for the purchase of its shares.

Noise: Investment noise is the twenty-four-hour flow of information surrounding Wall Street. TV news, the financial press, and even social media and gossip all contribute to the noise. "Ignore the noise, and your odds for success increase."[79]

Odd Lot: Stocks traded in units of under 100.

Off Board: A term used for securities not executed on a national securities exchange but, rather, over-the-counter.

Open-End Fund: An investment company that continually issues shares as it receives new capital or stands ready to redeem shares at net asset value.

---

78 Source: FINRA.org

79 Source: Rick Ferri, Forbes.com

Option: The right to buy or sell a stock at a specific price within a given time.

Over-the-counter: Method of issuing securities for those companies that may not meet the requirements for trading on the Big Board or their regional exchanges. The dealers may or may not be members of a securities exchange but must be members of the National Association of Security Dealers.

Penny stocks: Stocks selling at less than five dollars a share. These are mainly over-the-counter stocks and may be speculative.

Pension Plans: Also known as defined benefit retirement plans, these provide a specified amount of money after you retire following a set number of years of service (in other words, the benefit is "defined" in advance). Once you retire, the amount you receive is fixed and usually does not increase with inflation.

Portfolio: A portfolio is a collection of securities and other investments. Your "investment portfolio" refers to your investments within the plan.

Preferred stock: Stock promising prior claim on the company's earnings. Dividends are paid at a specified time before common stock shareholders receive theirs, and in case of liquidation, preferred stockholders have priority in all claims.

Price-earnings ratio: A formula whereby the cost of a stock is divided by its earnings for a 12-month period. XYZ common stock sells on the market for $30 and pays a $2 dividend. The price-earnings ratio is 15 to 1.

Prospectus: A prospectus provides investors with a thorough description of a mutual fund. It explains the fund's objective, how it invests its money, and describes fees and expenses associated with the fund. You should read a fund's prospectus before choosing your investment.

Return: This is the rate an investment earns (expressed as a percentage). It generally refers to the change in value (increase or decrease in share or unit price) and any income earned on the investment over a period. It's a way of comparing investments.

Securities: This term refers to all investment options (including stocks, bonds, and short-term securities) and shares of mutual funds, etc.

SIPC: Abbreviation of Securities Investor Protection Corporation, which provides funds (when necessary) to protect member firms' customers' equity.

Standard and Poor's Stock Price Index (S&P 500 Index): Similar to the Dow Jones Industrial Average, except that Standard and Poor uses not 30 industrial corporations but 500 major corporations consisting of industrials, railroads, and utilities, all listed on the New York Stock Exchange.

Stock: A company sells stock to raise money. When individuals or companies buy stocks, they become partial owners of the corporation issuing the stock. This ownership is called "equity."

Stock Split: Agreement voted by the directors of a corporation and approved by its shareholders to divide the outstanding shares into an increased number of shares, such as 2 for 1; the equity remains the same. Ann Smith owns 100 shares of XZ stock selling for $50 a share. After the 2-for-1 split, Ann Smith owns 200 shares of XZ stock at $25 a share.

Tax-deferred Contributions: The amount you choose to have deducted from your paycheck and contributed to your retirement savings plan.

Your contributions are deducted from your paycheck before income taxes are taken out, reducing your current taxable income. Taxes will be due when you withdraw money from your plan (generally after age 59½).

Tender offer: Request by a corporation (under specific terms and for a certain period) for the public and other stockholders (such as institutions) to surrender their stocks, usually at a price higher than the current market price.

Treasury Inflation Protected Securities (TIPS): TIPS are designed to protect investors against inflation risk. They are sold with maturities of 5, 10, or 30 years.

U.S. Government Marketable Securities: "The main difference between Treasury notes, bonds, and bills is length. Treasury notes have maturities of 2 to 10 years, Treasure bonds have maturities of 20 to 30 years, and Treasure bills have maturities between 4 and 52 weeks" (Quizlet.com).

U.S. Savings Bonds: The term that usually refers to a series of bonds issued by the federal government. Some series are discount type. The income from these bonds is taxable. Sometimes the government refers to these series by letters such as "E" and "H."

Yield: Yield is the effective interest rate or dividend a security pays to its investors.

Zero-Coupon Bond: A zero-coupon bond is a debt security that does not pay interest but instead trades at a discount. Much like a savings bond—you purchase a $50 bond for $25 and receive the full face amount upon maturity.

ONLINE COURSE

Want to learn more about how to become a great investor?

Visit greatinvestor.org/course to enroll in the Great Investor online course.

This insightful course will help you discover several investment strategies and techniques on how to improve your investment skills.

An investment in knowledge pays the best interest.
— BEN FRANKLIN

An intelligent heart acquires knowledge, and the ear of the wise seeks knowledge.
— PROVERBS 18:15

Best investment I ever made. Wish I had found this course years ago.
— DEBI F.

Richard's course was enlightening. Learning from someone with so much experience made a true difference in my own portfolio.
— SOLOMON T.

FREE RESOURCES AT GREATINVESTOR.ORG

Podcasts

Women and Investing

Stocks and the Stock Market

Investing

Annuities

Mutual Funds

Getting Your Financial House in Order

How to Get Sound Investment Advice

Bonds

Exchange-Traded Funds

Asset Allocation

Real Estate Investment Trusts

Behave Yourself

Long-Term Care

What Ever Happened to the Promised Land?

Ramsey vs. Reality

How to Be a Great Investor

6 Ways to Increase Your Monthly Income and 5 Ways to Lower Your Portfolio Taxes

Retirement Planning

Timeless Principles to Become a Better Investor

Free Downloads

20 Most Common Mistakes Retirees Make—and How to Avoid Them

The Women, Money + Power Study

Balancing God's Checkbook

Investing 101

Retirement Money Deserves a Good Home

What My Family Should Know

31 Timeless Principles for Investing Success

Common Sense Principles for Achieving Financial Independence

20 Practical and Easy Ways to Save Real Money

A Retiree's Guide to a Secure and Worry-Free Retirement

The Bible and Investing

6 Ways to Lower the Taxes on Investment Portfolios

God is in the Multiplication Business

6 Ways to Increase Your Monthly Income

A Critique on Primerica

10 Thought-provoking Ideas on What to Do with Your Required Minimum Distributions

A Dave Ramsey Manifesto

Additional Resources

Blog

Financial newsletter

FREE risk analysis

Financial tools and calculators

NEXT STEPS

Now that you've finished reading this book, here are some next steps for you to take:

1. Join the Community

Join our community and get early access to upcoming books. Visit our websites and follow us on social media for additional resources: articles, podcasts, and events to support your financial journey.

Sign up for our free financial newsletter at:

WWW.GREATINVESTOR.ORG

Follow and like us at:

www.facebook.com/-Great-Investor-201860620691284

Subscribe to the *How to Be a Great Investor* podcast available on iTunes and Google.

2. Share this Book

Tell others you think will enjoy this book. Spreading the word helps to reach new readers, grow this movement, and encourage the continued production of similar content.

Also, if you haven't yet read our other titles, now would be a good time to continue your quest to become a great investor.

3. Enroll in our Online Course

Visit greatinvestor.org/course to enroll. This insightful course will help you discover several investment strategies and techniques on how to improve your investment skills.

Visit
www.GreatInvestor.org

THANK YOU

ABOUT THE AUTHOR

Richard Everett has worked in the financial arena for over 35 years. Named Financial Planner of the Year in 1996 by First Financial Planners, Richard has taught financial courses to thousands of people via his radio and television shows, his books, and in person. Richard is also an internationally known speaker. He has presented biblically based financial principles in churches, conferences, Bible colleges, and universities, including the Yale University School of Management Believers in Business Conference.

DISCLAIMER

The financial information provided in this book is for informational purposes only and not for the purpose of providing specific financial advice. Investing carries the risk that you can potentially lose part or all of your money. Investors must independently and thoroughly research and analyze each and every investment before investing. Use of the information contained in this book does not create any financial advisory relationship with us. We are not responsible for your use or misuse of the educational material presented or any consequences thereof. You should contact a qualified financial advisor to obtain advice regarding any specific financial investing questions or concerns. Pursuant to IRS Circular 230, any tax advice provided in this book may not be used to avoid tax penalties or promote, market, or recommend any matter herein. The author expressly disclaims liability for any direct, indirect, incidental, special, or consequential damages or lost profits that result (directly or indirectly) from the use of the material herein. Always use caution and wisdom before investing.

I welcome comments and corrections through my website, www.GreatInvestor.org.